Fifth Edition

W9-BWG-079

Asking the Right Questions

A Guide to Critical Thinking

M. Neil Browne

Stuart M. Keeley

Bowling Green State University

Prentice Hall
Upper Saddle River, New Jersey 07458

Library of Congress Cataloging-in-Publication Data

Browne, M. Neil (date)
    Asking the right questions : a guide to critical thinking / M.
Neil Browne, Stuart M. Keeley. —5th ed.
        p.   cm.
    Includes index.
    ISBN 0-13-758186-6 9pbk.)
    1. Reading.   2. Criticism.   3. Critical thinking.   I. Keeley,
Stuart M. (date).   II. Title.
PN83.B785   1997
418'.4—dc21   97–25524
                                                        CIP

Editor-in-chief: Charlyce Jones Owen
Acquisitions editor: Maggie Barbieri
Editorial/production supervision and
    interior design: Mary Araneo
Buyer: Mary Ann Gloriande
Cover designer: Kiwi Design

This book was set in 10/12 New Baskerville by A & A
Publishing Services, Inc. and was printed by Courier
Companies, Inc. The cover was printed by Phoenix
Color Corp.

Printed in the United States of America

10   9   8   7   6

ISBN 0-13-758186-6

PRENTICE-HALL INTERNATIONAL (UK) LIMITED, *LONDON*
PRENTICE-HALL OF AUSTRALIA PTY. LIMITED, *SYDNEY*
PRENTICE-HALL CANADA INC., *TORONTO*
PRENTICE-HALL HISPANOAMERICANA, S.A., *MEXICO*
PRENTICE-HALL OF INDIA PRIVATE LIMITED, *NEW DELHI*
PRENTICE-HALL OF JAPAN, INC., *TOKYO*
PEARSON EDUCATION ASIA PTE. LTD., *SINGAPORE*
EDITORA PRENTICE-HALL DO BRASIL, LTDA., *RIO DE JANEIRO*

Contents

3   What Are the Reasons?   23

4   What Words or Phrases Are Ambiguous?   35

5   What Are the Value Conflicts and Assumptions?   51

10   Are There Rival Causes?   124

11   Are the Statistics Deceptive?   138

12   What Significant Information Is Omitted?   147

13   What Reasonable Conclusions Are Possible?   158

14   Practice and Review   169

Index   177

Preface

Previous editions of *Asking the Right Questions* have been welcome in hundreds of classrooms. Realizing that tens of thousands of learners have used our text to develop their critical-thinking abilities is both exhilarating and scary for us. We feel a major responsibility to earn anew the confidence of our readers. Toward that end we have maintained the basic structure of previous editions, while updating the illustrations and revising those sections that loyal readers have urged us to clarify or include.

This fifth edition is hence much more a joint work than the title page suggests. It is increasingly difficult for us to determine where our contributions end and where those of our readers begin. We hope that this edition reflects any wisdom that may have been lurking in former editions, while taking advantage of fresh insights gleaned from our own teaching and the caring suggestions of others.

Like this edition of *Asking the Right Questions*, critical thinking is both old and new. Systematic evaluation of arguments based on explicit rational criteria is as old as recorded history. Terminology changes, emphases emerge, and worthwhile disputes about the criteria for rational conversation break out. But the habit of questioning the quality of the reasoning for a belief or contention is implicit in our daily living.

Certainly, individuals may not be particularly skilled at this questioning process, but it is hard to imagine what it would mean to always and ever accept as true whatever we hear. Critical thinking thus has staying power. All of us can be confident that the interest in critical thinking will outlive us. So this book is part of a very old, yet enduring, tradition. Our interest in critical thinking ties us together in an important respect: We want to think carefully before we make a belief our own.

From the start of this book's history, we have been motivated by a variety of personal experiences and observations. First, we have been dismayed by the degree to which students and citizens in general increasingly depend on "experts"—textbook writers, teachers, lawyers, politicians, journalists, and TV commentators. As the complexity of the world seems to increase at an accelerating rate, there is a greater tendency to become passive absorbers of information, uncritically accepting what is seen and heard. We are concerned that too many of us are not actively making personal choices about what to accept and what to reject.

Thus, the need for such a book is now even more pronounced. The use of "sound bites," the popularity of simplistic arguments, and the amount of information to which we are exposed every day have all increased dramatically. To encourage us all to use critical thinking more frequently as an antidote to this "information explosion" is the dream of *Asking the Right Questions*.

Our experience in teaching critical-thinking skills to our students over a number of years has convinced us that when individuals with diverse abilities are taught these skills in a simplified format, they can learn to apply them successfully. In the process, they develop greater confidence in their ability to make rational choices about social issues, even those with which they have formerly had little experience.

Another motivating factor for the book has been our inability to find materials with which to teach the skills we wanted students to learn. We did not want a philosophy text, but rather a book that, while informal in nature, would outline basic critical-thinking skills explicitly, concisely, and simply. We did not find such a book.

Thus, we have written a text that does a number of things that other books have failed to do. This text develops an integrated series of question-asking skills that can be applied widely. These skills are discussed in an informal style. (We have written to a general audience, not to any specialized group.)

The development of *Asking the Right Questions* has leaned heavily on our joint experience of 50 years as teachers of critical thinking. Our ideas have evolved in response to numerous classroom experiences with students at many different levels, from freshman to Ph.D. students.

These experiences have taught us certain emphases that are particularly effective in learning critical thinking. For instance, we provide many opportunities for the readers to apply their skills and to receive immediate feedback following the practice application. The book is replete with examples of writing devoted to controversial contemporary topics. The breadth of topics introduces the average reader to numerous controversies with which he or she may have little familiarity. The book is coherently organized, in that critical questions are discussed sequentially as the reader progresses from understanding to evaluating. In addition, it integrates cognitive and value dimensions—a very important aspect of critical thinking and personal decision making.

One feature that deserves to be highlighted is the applicability of *Asking the Right Questions* to numerous life experiences extending far beyond the classroom. The habits and attitudes associated with critical thinking are transferable to consumer, medical, legal, and general ethical choices. When our surgeon says surgery is needed, it can be life sustaining to seek answers to critical questions.

To make this general applicability apparent and to provide an element of cohesiveness to the book, each chapter begins with brief exchanges concerning the desirability of capital punishment. We all care about this issue, and critical thinking enables us to express our concerns in a more reasonable fashion. The exchange should be read both before and after the applicable chapter. It is our hope that the second reading will be more satisfying.

In addition, the fifth edition includes the following new features:

1. *Caution Boxes* that warn readers of common misunderstandings that interfere with the effective use of an idea or skill. These are set off in the text by dynamite sticks and a long fuse encasing the cautions.
2. Expanded use of graphics and cartoons to provide a livelier presentation format and to clarify complex or significant points.
3. Revision of almost half of the practice passages to reflect changing student interests.
4. Highlighting of key definitions of critical-thinking terminology.

Each new element has emerged from the teaching experience of numerous colleagues.

Who would find *Asking the Right Questions* especially beneficial? Because of our teaching experiences with readers representing many different levels of ability, we have difficulty envisioning any academic course or program for which this book would not be useful. In fact, the first four editions have been used in law, English, pharmacy, philosophy, education, psychology, sociology, religion, and social science courses.

A few uses for the book seem especially appropriate. Teachers in general education programs may want to begin their courses by assigning it as a coherent response to their students' requests to explain what is expected of them. English courses that emphasize expository writing could use this text both as a format for evaluating arguments prior to constructing an essay and as a checklist of problems that the writer should attempt to avoid as he or she writes. The book is especially functional in courses for training prospective teachers and graduate assistants because it makes explicit much that teachers will want to encourage in their students. Courses in study-skill development may be enriched by supplementing their current content with our step-by-step description of the process of critical reading and thinking. The text can also be used as the central focus of courses designed specifically to teach critical reading and thinking skills.

While *Asking the Right Questions* stems primarily from our classroom experiences, it is written so that it can guide the reading and listening habits of almost everyone. The skills that it seeks to develop are those that any critical reader needs in order for reading to serve as a basis for rational decisions. The critical questions stressed in the book can enhance anyone's reasoning, regardless of the extent of his or her formal education.

This fifth edition owes special debts to many people. Many readers of earlier editions have cared enough about this project to suggest improvements. Several have been especially helpful. As always, Andrea Giampetro-Meyer of Loyola College in Baltimore has provided us with much dependable advice. We also wish to acknowledge the following Prentice Hall reviewers: Beth M. Waggenspack of Virginia Tech, Donald Heidt of the College of the Canyons, Barbara Fowler of Longview Community College, and Verlyne Starr of Oakland Community College.

While our students are always a major source of suggested improvements, a few distinguished themselves in that regard. The fifth edition depended heavily on improvements suggested by Carrie Williamson, whose concern for quality is extraordinary.

M. Neil Browne
Stuart M. Keeley

1

The Benefit of Asking the Right Questions

Introduction

Each of us is bombarded with information. Every day we encounter new facts and opinions. In text books, newspapers, magazines, and on the Internet, writers present ideas they want us to accept. One social scientist tells us violence on television is bad for young people; another tells us it does no harm. One economist argues for reducing taxes to stem inflation; another argues that we should increase interest rates. One educational critic recommends eliminating the "frills," such as foreign language and physical education requirements; another recommends we expand such "necessities."

In all areas of knowledge there are issues about which experts in those fields disagree. You as a reader have the tough job of deciding which authority to believe. Whether you are reading a nursing journal, a critique of a poem, a textbook, or even the sports page, you will be faced with the problem of deciding which conclusions to accept, which to reject, and which to withhold judgment on.

As a thoughtful person you must make a choice about how you will react to what you see and hear. One alternative is to accept passively what you encounter; doing so automatically results in your making someone else's opinion your own. A more active alternative consists of asking questions of yourself in an effort to reach a personal decision about the worth of what you have experienced. This book is written for those who prefer the second alternative.

Critical Thinking to the Rescue

Listening and reading critically—that is, reacting with systematic evaluation to what you have heard and read—requires a set of skills and attitudes. These skills and attitudes are built around a series of critical questions.

We could have expressed them as a list of things you should do, but a system of questions is more consistent with the spirit of curiosity, wonder, and intellectual adventure essential to critical thinking. Thinking carefully is always an unfinished project, a story looking for an ending that will never arrive. Critical questions provide a structure for critical thinking that supports a continual, ongoing search for better opinions, decisions, or judgments.

Consequently, *critical thinking*, as we will use the term, refers to the following:

1. awareness of a set of interrelated critical questions,
2. ability to ask and answer critical questions at appropriate times, and
3. desire to actively use the critical questions.

The goal of this book is to encourage you in all three of these dimensions.

Questions require the other person to do something. We are saying to them: I am curious; I want to know more; help me. This request shows respect for the other person. You really want to understand what he or she is saying. The point of your questions is that you need her help to have a deeper understanding or appreciation of her reasoning.

The critical questions will be shared with you bit by bit, one question at a time. As a package, they will be useful whenever you choose to react to what you are hearing or reading. This book will guide you through the critical questions so you can recognize their benefit to every thinking person.

These skills and attitudes will be especially helpful to you as a student and as a citizen. As a student, they should be useful whenever you are asked to:

1. react critically to an essay or to evidence presented in a textbook,
2. judge the quality of a lecture or speech,
3. form an argument,
4. write an essay based on a reading assignment, or
5. participate in class.

Attention: Critical thinking consists of an awareness of a set of interrelated critical questions, plus the ability and willingness to ask and answer them at appropriate times.

As a citizen, you should find them especially helpful in shaping your voting behavior and your purchasing decisions, as well as improving your self-confidence by increasing your sense of intellectual independence.

The Sponge and Panning for Gold: Alternative Thinking Styles

One approach to thinking is similar to the way in which a sponge reacts to water: by *absorbing*. This commonly used approach has some clear advantages.

First, the more information you absorb about the world, the more capable you are of understanding its complexities. Knowledge you have acquired provides a foundation for more complicated thinking later. For instance, it would be very difficult to judge the value of a sociological theory before you had absorbed a core of knowledge about sociology.

A second advantage of the sponge approach is that it is relatively passive. Rather than requiring strenuous mental effort, it tends to be rather quick and easy, especially when the material is presented in a clear and interesting fashion. The primary mental effort involves concentration and memory.

While absorbing information provides a productive start toward becoming a thoughtful person, the sponge approach has a serious disadvantage: It provides no method for deciding which information and opinions to believe and which to reject. If a reader relied on the sponge approach all the time, she would believe whatever she read *last*.

We think you would rather choose for yourself what to absorb and what to ignore. To make this choice, you must read with a special attitude—a question-asking attitude. Such a thinking style requires active participation. The writer is trying to speak to you, and you should try to talk back to him, even though he is not present.

We call this interactive approach the *panning-for-gold* style of thinking. Gold is a soft, bright yellow metal that has been highly valued since prehistoric times. It is found in most parts of the world, but almost always in low concentrations. As a result, finding it is a challenging and difficult task.

The process of panning for gold provides a model for active readers and listeners as they try to determine the worth of what they read and hear. The task is challenging and sometimes tedious, but the reward can be tremendous. To distinguish the gold from the gravel in a conversation requires you to ask frequent questions and to reflect about the answers.

The sponge approach emphasizes knowledge acquisition; the panning-for-gold approach stresses active interaction with knowledge as it is being acquired. Thus, the two approaches can complement each other. To pan for intellectual gold, there must be something in your pan to evaluate. To evaluate arguments we must possess knowledge.

Approaches to Learning

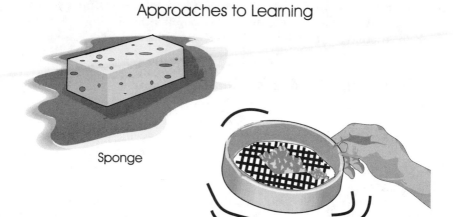

Sponge

Panning-for-gold

Let us more closely examine how the two approaches lead to different behavior. What does the individual who takes the sponge approach do when he reads material? He reads sentences carefully, trying to remember as much as he can. He may underline or highlight key words and sentences. He may take notes summarizing the major topics and major points. He checks his underlining or notes to be sure he is not forgetting anything important. His mission is to find and understand what the author has to say. He memorizes the reasoning but doesn't evaluate it.

What does the reader who takes the panning-for-gold approach do? Like the person using the sponge approach, he approaches his reading with the hope that he will acquire new knowledge. Then the similarity ends. The panning-for-gold approach requires that the reader ask himself a number of questions to clarify logical steps in the material and to help identify important omissions. The reader who uses the panning-for-gold approach frequently questions *why* the author makes various claims. He writes notes to himself in the margins indicating problems with the reasoning. He continually interacts with the material. His intent is to critically evaluate the material and formulate personal conclusions based on the evaluation.

An Example of the Panning-for-Gold Approach

A major enduring issue in American society concerns what kind of gun control laws we need. Let's look at one position on this issue. Try to decide whether the argument is convincing.

> Arguments for banning guns are mostly myths, and what we need now is not more laws, but more law enforcement. One myth is that most murderers are ordinary,

law-abiding citizens who kill a relative or acquaintance in a moment of anger only because a gun is available. In fact, every study of homicide shows the overwhelming majority of murderers are career criminals, people with lifelong histories of violence. The typical murderer has a prior criminal history averaging at least six years, with four major felony arrests.

Another myth is that gun owners are ignorant rednecks given to senseless violence. However, studies consistently show that, on the average, gun owners are better educated and have more prestigious jobs than nonowners. To judge by their applications for permits to carry guns at all times, the following are (or were) gun owners: Eleanor Roosevelt, Joan Rivers, Robert Goulet, Leland DuPont, Arthur Godfrey, Sammy Davis Jr., Donald Trump, John Foster Dulles, and John, Laurance, David Winthrop, and Nelson Rockefeller.

A third myth is that the Second Amendment protects only the states' right to arm a militia. But this interpretation is recent. Significantly, the two earliest commentaries on the Second Amendment, which were before Congress when it passed the Bill of Rights, described it as guaranteeing to the people "their right to keep and bear their private arms" (Tinch Coxe) and "their own arms" (Sam Adams). To James Madison, author of the Second Amendment, "the advantage that the Americans have over every other nation is that they are armed."

A fourth myth is that guns are not useful for self-defense. On the contrary! Every study has shown that handguns are used more often in repelling crimes than in committing them. While handguns are used in about 581,000 crimes yearly, they are used to repel about 645,000 crimes.

The emphasis on changing gun laws is fundamentally diversionary. In the premier criminological study of gun control enforcement, Bendis and Balkin conclude: "It is very possible that if gun laws do potentially reduce gun-related crime, the present laws are all that are needed if they are enforced. What good would stronger laws do when the courts have demonstrated that they will not enforce them?"[1]

If you apply the sponge approach to the passage, you probably will try to remember the reasons that we don't need further controls on guns. If so, you will have absorbed some knowledge. However, how convinced should you be by the above reasons? You can't evaluate them until you have applied the panning-for-gold approach to the passage—that is, until you have asked the right questions.

By asking the right questions, you would discover a number of possible weaknesses in the communicator's arguments. For instance, you might be concerned about all of the following:

1. What does the author mean by "overwhelming majority" or by "typical

---

[1]Adapted from D. Kates, Jr. and P. Harris, "How to Make Their Day," *National Review* (October 21, 1991), p. 30–32.

murderer"? Is the minority still a substantial number of murderers who kill relatives in a moment of anger?

2. What is meant by "gun owners"? Are they the ones who buy the kind of guns that gun control advocates are trying to ban?

3. How adequate were the cited research studies? Were the samples sufficiently large, random, and diverse from which to generalize widely?

4. Has the author lied with statistics by impressing us with large, rather precise numbers, like 581,000 and 645,000? What is the basis for these numbers? Can we rely on them?

5. How much reliance should we place on the authorities Bendis and Balkin? How reliable and selective is the information they have access to?

6. What possible benefits of gun control are not mentioned? Have important studies that disagree with the author's position been omitted?

7. Can we assume that the earliest commentaries on the Second Amendment were thus the "right" commentaries? What were later commentaries? How well argued were they?

8. Is it legitimate to assume that because some famous people own guns, then owning guns is desirable? Do these people have special expertise concerning the pros and cons of gun ownership?

9. To what extent are the author's arguments influenced by preferring the value of individual rights over community safety? Has that value preference influenced the interpretation of the data?

10. How many people are killed each year by handguns who would not have been killed were such guns not available?

If you want to ask these kinds of questions, this book is especially for you. Its primary purpose is to help you know when and how to ask questions that will enable you to decide what to believe.

The most important characteristic of the panning-for-gold approach is *interactive involvement*—a dialogue between the writer and the reader, or the speaker and the listener.

Clearly, there are times when the sponge approach is appropriate. Most of you have used it regularly and have acquired some level of success with it. It is much less likely that you are in the habit of employing the panning-for-gold approach—in part, simply because you have not had the training and practice. This book will not only help you ask the right questions, but will also provide frequent opportunities for practicing their use.

Panning for Gold: Asking Critical Questions

It would be nice if what other people were really saying were always obvious, if all their essential thoughts were clearly labeled for us, if the writer or speaker never made an error in his or her reasoning, and if all knowledgeable people agreed about answers to important questions. If this were the case, we could read and listen passively and let others do our thinking for us. However, the true state of affairs is quite the opposite. A person's reasoning is often not obvious. Important elements are often missing. Many elements that *are* present are unclear. Other elements that are present do not even belong there. Consequently, critical reading and listening are sorting processes through which you identify what makes sense and distinguish this clear thinking from the sloppy thinking that characterizes much of what you will encounter.

What's the point? The inadequacies in what someone says will not always leap out at you. You must be an *active* searcher. You can do this by *asking questions*. The best search strategy is a critical-questioning strategy. Throughout the book we will be showing you why certain critical questions are so important to ask. A powerful advantage of these questions is that they permit you to ask searching questions even when you know very little about the topic being discussed. For example, you do not need to be an expert on child care to ask critical questions about the adequacy of day-care centers.

The Myth of the "Right Answer"

Our ability to find definite answers to questions often depends on the type of question that puzzles us. Scientific questions about the physical world are the most likely to have answers that reasonable people will accept, because the physical world is in certain ways more dependable or predictable than the social world. While the precise distance to the moon or the age of a newly discovered bone from an ancient civilization may not be absolutely certain, agreement about the dimensions of our physical environment is widespread. Thus, in the physical sciences, we frequently can arrive at "the right answer."

Questions about human behavior are different. The causes of human behavior are so complex and so difficult to apply high standards of evidence to that we frequently cannot do much more than form intelligent guesses about why or when certain behavior will occur. In addition, because many of us care a great deal about explanations and descriptions of human behavior, we prefer that explanations or descriptions of the rate of abortion, the frequency of unemployment, or the causes of child abuse be consistent with what we want to believe. Hence we bring our preferences to any discussion of those issues and resist arguments that are inconsistent with them.

Since human behavior is so controversial and complex, the best answers that we can find for many questions about our behavior will be probabilistic in nature, lacking a high degree of certainty. Even if we are aware of all the evidence available about the effects of running on our mental health, the nature of such questions about human behavior will prevent our discovering the *exact truth* about such effects.

Regardless of the type of questions being asked, the issues that require your closest scrutiny are usually those about which "reasonable people" disagree. In fact, many issues are interesting exactly because there is strong disagreement about how to resolve them. Any controversy involves more than one position. Several positions may be supported with good reasons. Thus, when you engage in critical thinking, you should be seeking the position that seems most reasonable to you. There will seldom be a position on a social controversy about which you will be able to say, "This is clearly the right position on the issue." If such certainty were possible, reasonable people would not be debating the issue. Our focus in this book will be on such social controversies.

Even though you will not necessarily arrive at the "right answer" to social controversies, this book is designed to give you the skills to develop your best and most reasonable answer, given the nature of the problem and the available information. Decisions usually must be made in the face of uncertainty. Often we will not have the time or the ability to discover many of the important facts about a decision we must make. For example, it is simply unwise to ask all the right questions when someone you love is complaining of sharp chest pains and wants you to transport him to the emergency room.

Thinking and Feeling

When you first encounter a conclusion, you do so with a history. You have learned to care about certain things, to support particular interests, and to discount claims of a particular type. So you always start to think critically in the midst of existing opinions. You have emotional commitments to these existing opinions. They are *your* opinions, and you quite understandably feel protective of them.

However, if you are to grow, you need to recognize these feelings, and, as much as you are able, put them on a shelf for a bit. Only that effort will enable you to listen carefully when others offer arguments that threaten or violate your current beliefs. This openness is important because many of our own positions on issues are not especially reasonable ones; they are opinions given to us by others, and over many years we develop emotional attachments to them. Indeed, we frequently believe that we are being personally attacked when someone presents a conclusion contrary to our own. The danger of being emotionally involved in an issue prior to any active thought about it is that you may fail to consider potential good reasons for other positions—reasons that might be sufficient to change your mind on the issue if you would only listen to them.

Remember: Emotional involvement alone should not be the basis for accepting or rejecting a position. Ideally, emotional involvement should be most intense *after* reasoning has occurred. Thus, when you read, try to avoid letting emotional involvement cut you off from the reasoning of those with whom you initially disagree. A successful active learner is one who is willing to change his or her mind. If you are ever to change your mind, you must be as open as possible to ideas that strike you as weird or dangerous when you first encounter them.

Critical thinkers, however, are not machines. They care greatly about many issues. The depth of that concern can be seen in their willingness to do all the hard mental work associated with critical thinking. But any passion felt by critical thinkers is moderated by the recognition that their current beliefs are open to revision.

Caution: As part of the human tendency to dichotomize or think in extremes, those who emphasize critical thinking as an educational necessity sometimes express contempt for emotions. All of us know that unrestrained feelings can get us into trouble. They seem to encourage us to act first and think later. But any tool can be misused. Emotions are an invaluable aspect of each of us. Many of the feelings we have are the result of deep thought. We get angry at certain behavior for some very good reasons. We may admire specific people for some powerful reasons. So how should you feel about your feelings as you try to think critically? Our advice is to recognize your feelings to the extent possible, respect those that are the result of careful reflection, and try, as best you can, to prevent others from cluttering your reasoning.

DYNAMITE

Efficiency of Asking the Question, "Who Cares?"

Asking good questions is difficult but rewarding work. Some controversies will be much more important to you than others. When the consequences of a controversy for you and your community are minimal, you will want to spend less time and energy thinking critically about it than about more important controversies. For example, it makes sense to critically evaluate arguments for and against the protection of endangered species, because different positions on this issue lead to important consequences for society. It makes less sense to devote energy to evaluating whether blue is the favorite color of most corporate executives.

Your time is valuable. Before taking the time to critically evaluate an issue, ask the question, "Who cares?"

Weak-Sense and Strong-Sense Critical Thinking

Previous sections mentioned that you already have opinions about many personal and social issues. You are willing right now to take a position on such questions as should prostitution be legalized, is alcoholism a disease or willful misconduct, or was Ronald Reagan a successful president. You bring these initial opinions to what you hear and read.

Critical thinking can be used to either (1) defend *or* (2) evaluate and revise your initial beliefs. Professor Richard Paul's distinction between weak-sense and strong-sense critical thinking helps us appreciate these two antagonistic uses of critical thinking.

If you approach critical thinking as a method for defending your initial beliefs or those you are paid to have, you are engaged in weak-sense critical thinking. Why is it *weak?* To use critical-thinking skills in this manner is to be unconcerned with moving toward truth or virtue. The purpose of weak-sense critical thinking is to resist and annihilate opinions and reasoning different from yours. To see domination and victory over those who disagree with you as the objective of critical thinking is to ruin the potentially humane and progressive aspects of critical thinking.

In contrast, strong-sense critical thinking requires us to apply the critical questions to all claims, including our own. By forcing ourselves to look critically at our initial beliefs, we help protect against self-deception and conformity. It's easy to just stick with current beliefs, particularly when they are shared by many people. But when we take this easy road, we run the strong risk of making mistakes we could otherwise avoid.

Strong-sense critical thinking does not necessarily force us to give up our initial beliefs. It can provide a basis for strengthening those very beliefs, for understanding through reflection why they *do* make sense. A long time ago, John Stuart Mill warned us of the emptiness of a set of opinions accumulated without the help of strong-sense critical thinking:

> He who knows only his side of the case knows little of that. His reasons may have been good, and no one may have been able to refute them. But if he is equally unable to refute the reasons on the opposite side he has no ground for preferring either opinion.

To feel proud of a particular opinion it should be one we have selected—selected from alternative opinions that we have understood and evaluated.

The Satisfaction of Using the Panning-for-Gold Approach

Doing is usually more fun than watching; doing well is more fun than simply doing. If you start using the interactive process taught in this book, you can feel the same sense of pride in your reading and listening that you normally get from successful participation in physical activities.

Attention: Weak-sense critical thinking is the use of critical thinking to defend your current beliefs. Strong-sense critical thinking is the use of the same skills to evaluate all claims and beliefs, **especially your own.**

Critical thinkers find it satisfying to know when to say "no" to an idea or opinion and to know why that response is appropriate. If you regularly use the panning-for-gold approach, then anything that gets into your head will have been systematically examined first. When an idea or belief *does* pass the criteria developed here, it will make sense to agree with it—at least until new evidence appears.

Imagine how good you will feel if you know *why* you should ignore or accept a particular bit of advice. Frequently, those faced with an opinion different from their own respond by saying, "oh, that's just your opinion." But the issue should not be whose opinion it is, but rather whether it is a good opinion. Armed with the critical questions discussed in this book, you can experience the satisfaction of knowing why certain advice is nonsense.

The sponge approach is often satisfying because it permits you to accumulate information. Though this approach is productive, there is much more gratification in being a participant in a meaningful dialogue with the writer or speaker. Reading and listening become much richer as you begin to see things that others may have missed. As you question the correctness of reasoning, you will start to go beyond what someone wants you to believe. No one wants to be at the mercy of the last "expert" he meets. As you learn to select information and opinions systematically, you will probably desire to read more and more in a lifelong effort to decide which advice makes sense. The sponge approach works well on *Jeopardy*, but is a clumsy method for answering important questions in our lives.

Trying Out *New* Answers

Although there is often no absolutely right answer, this book tries to encourage your search for better answers. Certainly, some answers are more accurate, appropriate, useful, or moral than are others. For you to want to do the hard work necessary to find better answers, you need substantial curiosity and even courage.

Courage is required because to keep looking for better answers, we have to be willing to give up our current beliefs or positions. When we encounter a question, we probably already have an answer. Suppose someone says something to us about the appropriateness of behavior by animal-rights activists. In all probability we already have an opinion about the matter.

We don't listen to someone's argument with a blank slate. We feel a sense of ownership about opinions we call our own. It often takes incredible courage to give up on an opinion we have held for some time after listening to someone else. As critical thinkers, we have to struggle to force ourselves to try out new answers. The interplay between our old answers and new ones provides a basis for our growth.

Effective Communication and Critical Thinking

Many of the skills you will learn as you become a more critical thinker will improve the quality of your writing and speaking. As you write and speak, it helps to be aware of the expectations careful thinkers will have. Because your objective is communication, many of the questions the thoughtful person will ask in evaluating your writing or speech should serve as guides for your discourse. Several of the critical questions that we urge you to ask highlight problems you will want to avoid as you write or speak.

While the emphasis in this book is on effective thinking, the link to competent communication is so direct that it will be a theme throughout. Wherever appropriate, we will mention how the skill being encouraged is an aid to improved communication.

The Importance of Practice

Learning new critical-thinking skills is a lot like learning new physical skills. You cannot learn simply by being told what to do or by watching others. You have to practice, and frequently the practice will be both rewarding and hard work. Our goal is to make your learning as simple as possible. However, acquiring the habit of critical thinking will initially take a lot of practice.

The practice exercises and sample responses at the end of each chapter are an important part of this text. Try to do the exercises and only then compare your answers with ours. Our answers are not necessarily the only correct ones, but they provide illustrations of how to apply the question-asking skills.

The Right Questions

To give you an initial sense of the skills that *Asking the Right Questions* will help you acquire, we will list the critical questions for you here. By the end of the book, you should know when and how to ask these questions productively:

1. What are the issues and the conclusions?
2. What are the reasons?
3. What words or phrases are ambiguous?
4. What are the value conflicts and assumptions?
5. What are the descriptive assumptions?
6. Are there any fallacies in the reasoning?
7. How good is the evidence?
8. Are there rival causes?
9. Are the statistics deceptive?
10. What significant information is omitted?
11. What reasonable conclusions are possible?

2

What Are the Issue and the Conclusion?

Before we evaluate someone's reasoning, we must first find it. Doing so sounds simple; it isn't. To get started as a critical thinker, you must practice the identification of the issue and the conclusion.

Fraternities and sororities are often involved in charitable activities. They provide volunteers to raise money for many worthwhile causes. Their contribution in this regard deserves our praise.

Yet we cannot stop our description of Greek organizations with this incomplete picture. Their good deeds are overwhelmed by their encouragement of conformity, childish pranks, and anti-intellectual antics. The abundant talents of their members should be channeled elsewhere.

The person who wrote this assessment of Greek organizations very much wants you to believe something. In general, those who create editorials, books, magazine articles, or speeches are trying to alter your perceptions or beliefs. For you to form a reasonable reaction, you must first identify the controversy or *issue* as well as the thesis or *conclusion* being pushed onto you. (Someone's *conclusion* is his or her intended message to you. Its purpose is to shape your beliefs and/or behavior.) Otherwise, you will be reacting to a distorted version of the attempted communication.

When you have completed this chapter, you should be able to answer the first of our critical questions successfully:

☞   *Critical Question:*   **What are the issue and the conclusion?**

Kinds of Issues

It will be helpful at this point to identify two kinds of issues you will typically encounter. The following questions illustrate one of these:

> **Do** obese people have more emotional problems than nonobese people?
>
> **What** causes AIDS?
>
> **Who** won the presidential debate?
>
> **How much will** college cost in the year 2010?
>
> **Can** a child's IQ be raised by a stimulating environment?
>
> **Does** watching violence on TV make us relatively insensitive to crime on the streets?

All these questions have one thing in common. They demand answers that attempt to describe the way the world is, was, or is going to be. For example, answers to the first two questions might be, "In general, obese people have more emotional problems," and "A particular virus causes AIDS."

We will refer to such issues as *descriptive issues.* You will find such issues all around you. They appear in textbooks of such disciplines as psychology, soci-

---

Attention: An issue is a question or controversy that is responsible for the conversation or discussion. It is the stimulus for what is being said.

Attention: A conclusion is the message that the speaker or writer wishes you to receive and accept.

Attention: Descriptive issues are those that raise questions about the accuracy of descriptions of the past, present, or future.

---

ology, political science, economics, education, and geography, in magazines, on the Internet, and on television. Such issues reflect our curiosity about patterns or order in the world.

Now let's look at examples of a second kind of question:

Should capital punishment be abolished?

Is it desirable to fluoridate drinking water?

What ought to be done about unemployment?

Should people be required to retire at a certain age?

All of these questions demand answers that suggest the way the world *ought to be*. For example, answers to the first two questions might be, "Capital punishment *should be* abolished," and "We *ought* to fluoridate our drinking water."

These issues are ethical, or moral, issues; they raise questions about what is right or wrong, desirable or undesirable, good or bad. They demand prescriptive answers. Thus, we will refer to these issues as *prescriptive issues*. Social controversies are often prescriptive issues—that is, those surrounding abortion, marijuana, handguns, pornography, prostitution, and the protection of our environment.

We have somewhat oversimplified. Sometimes it will be quite difficult to decide what kind of issue is being discussed. It will be useful to keep these distinctions in mind, however, because the kinds of critical evaluations you eventually make will differ depending on the kind of issue to which you are responding.

What Is the Issue?

How does one go about determining the basic question or issue? Sometimes it is very simple: The writer or speaker will tell you. The issue may be identified in the body of the text, usually right at the beginning, or it may even be found in the title. If the issue is explicitly stated, you will usually find phrases such as the following:

The question I am raising is whether taxes are too high in our country.

Reducing the speed limit: *Is it the right thing to do?*

Should sex education be taught in the school?

Why isn't our present educational system working?

Does how you sleep reveal your personality?

Attention: Prescriptive issues are those that raise questions about what we should do or what is right or wrong, good or bad.

Unfortunately, the question is not always explicitly stated and instead must be inferred from the conclusion. In such cases the conclusion must be found before you can identify the issue. Thus, where the question is not explicitly stated, the first step in critical evaluation is to find the conclusion—a frequently difficult step.

We cannot critically evaluate until we find the conclusion!

Let's see how we go about looking for that very important structural element.

Searching for the Author's or Speaker's Conclusion

To identify the conclusion, the critical thinker must ask, "What is the writer or speaker trying to prove?" or "What is the communicator's main point?" The answer to this question will be the conclusion.

In searching for a conclusion, you will be looking for a statement or set of statements that the writer or speaker wants you to believe. She wants you to believe the conclusion on the basis of her other statements. In short, the basic structure of persuasive communication or argument is: *This* because of *that*. *This* refers to the conclusion; *that* refers to the support for the conclusion. This structure represents the process of *inference*.

Conclusions are *inferred;* they are derived from reasoning. Conclusions are ideas that require other ideas to support them. Thus, whenever someone claims something is true or ought to be done and provides no statements to support his claim, that claim is *not* a conclusion because no one has offered any basis for belief. In contrast, unsupported claims are what we refer to as *mere* opinions.

The last paragraph says a lot. It would be a good idea for you to read it again. Understanding the nature of a conclusion is an essential step toward critical reading and listening. Let's look closely at a conclusion and at the inference process. Here is a brief paragraph; see whether you can identify the conclusion, then the statements that support it.

> We oppose a mandatory retirement age. We believe that age is an inappropriate and unreasonable basis for determining whether an individual can do a job.

The statement "We oppose a mandatory retirement age" is this writer's answer to the question of whether there should be a mandatory retirement age; it is her conclusion. She supports the conclusion (a belief) with another belief: "We believe that age is an inappropriate and unreasonable basis for determining whether an individual can do a job." Do you see why the later belief is not a conclusion? It is not the conclusion because it is used to prove something else. *Remember:* To believe one statement (the conclusion) because you think it is well supported by *other* beliefs is to make an inference. When people engage in this process, they are reasoning; the conclusion is the outcome of this reasoning.

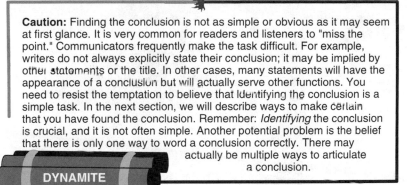

Caution: Finding the conclusion is not as simple or obvious as it may seem at first glance. It is very common for readers and listeners to "miss the point." Communicators frequently make the task difficult. For example, writers do not always explicitly state their conclusion; it may be implied by other statements or the title. In other cases, many statements will have the appearance of a conclusion but will actually serve other functions. You need to resist the temptation to believe that Identifying the conclusion is a simple task. In the next section, we will describe ways to make certain that you have found the conclusion. Remember: *Identifying* the conclusion is crucial, and it is not often simple. Another potential problem is the belief that there is only one way to word a conclusion correctly. There may actually be multiple ways to articulate a conclusion.

DYNAMITE

Clues to Discovery: How to Find the Conclusion

There are a number of clues to help you identify the conclusion.

CLUE No. 1: **Ask what the issue is.** Because a conclusion is always a response to an issue, it will help you find the conclusion if you know the issue. We discussed earlier how to identify the issue. First, look at the title. Next, look at the opening paragraphs. If this technique doesn't help, skimming several pages may be necessary.

CLUE No. 2: **Look for indicator words.** The conclusion will frequently be preceded by *indicator words* that announce a conclusion is coming. A list of such indicator words follows:

therefore	instead
thus	we may deduce that
but	points to the conclusion that
so	the point I'm trying to make is
hence	in my opinion
in short	the most obvious explanation
it follows that	it is highly probable that
it is believed that	in fact
shows that	the truth of the matter is
indicates that	alas
suggests that	as a result
proves that	it should be clear that
yet	

When you see these indicator words, take note of them. They tell you that a conclusion may follow.

Read the following two passages; then identify and highlight the indicator words. By doing so, you will have identified the statements containing the conclusion.

Passage A

But now, more than two years after voters overwhelmingly approved the lottery, it has been proven that the game is not a sure success; in fact, it can be considered a failure.

First of all, during the campaign for passage of the lottery, the public was repeatedly told that the proceeds would go toward curing the financial ills of both higher education and local primary and secondary schools. It was on this premise that the lottery received overwhelming support from the public. Not until it was approved, however, was it widely conceded that lottery profits would go into the general fund instead of the state's education budget. Less than half of the lottery's profits goes to education.

Passage B

When mothers smoke during pregnancy, it is highly probable that their children will read with less comprehension when they attend school. A recent study of 10,000 children born in the 1970s suggests that there is a small but statistically significant reduction in reading-comprehension scores of children whose mothers smoked when they were pregnant.

You should have highlighted the following phrases: *but, it has been proven,* and *in fact* in Passage A, and *it is highly probable that* in Passage B. The conclusions follow these words.

Unfortunately, many written and spoken communications do not introduce the conclusion with indicator words. However, when *you* write, you should draw attention to your thesis with indicator words. Those words act as a neon sign, drawing attention to the thesis you want the reader to accept.

CLUE No. 3: **Look in likely locations.** Conclusions tend to occupy certain locations. The first two places to look are at the beginning and at the end. Many writers begin with a statement of purpose, which contains what they are trying to prove. Others summarize their conclusions at the end. If you are reading a long, complex passage and are having difficulty seeing where it is going, skip ahead to the ending.

CLUE No. 4: **Remember what a conclusion is not.** Conclusions will not be any of the following:

Examples

Statistics

Definitions

Background information

Evidence

When you have identified the conclusion, check to see that it is none of these.

Caution: If you miss the conclusion, you will simply be "spinning your wheels" as you try to evaluate critically. Missing the point not only leads to frustration but frequently to unnecessary arguments. All subsequent critical-questioning techniques require correct identification of the conclusion. When you have identified it, highlight it in some way. You will need to refer back to it several times as you ask further questions. As you critically evaluate, always keep the conclusion in mind.

DYNAMITE

Your Thesis and Effective Writing

Since readers of *your* writing will be looking for your thesis or conclusion, help them by giving it the clarity it deserves. It is the central message you want to deliver. Emphasize it; leave no doubt about what it actually is. Making your conclusion easily identifiable not only makes a reader's task easier, it also may improve the logic of your writing. By requiring yourself to define a thesis, you are more likely to provide reasoning that moves toward the single goal of a convincing conclusion. An effective way to emphasize the conclusion is to insert it at the beginning or end of your essay and precede it with an indicator word.

Practice Exercises

☞   *Critical Question:* ***What are the issue and the conclusion?***

In the following passages locate the issue and conclusion. As you search, be sure to look for indicator words.

Passage 1

Day-care centers and babysitters are becoming more and more popular as greater numbers of women enter the workforce. Although mothers may enjoy working outside the home, they might be harming their children when they hand them over to someone else for care during work hours.

This current trend means that some women return to their workplace very soon after a child has been born. Although job requirements may prompt this hasty return to the workforce, women must reevaluate their priorities. Having a child is a major responsibility, and women must realize that children must come first.

Who can provide the love and attention that young children desperately need for their emotional and physical development? While a babysitter might feel affection for a child, only a mother could offer her child unconditional love and encouragement. Also, children do not get as much individual attention at day-care centers.

While a job might provide extra money for a household, mothers must realize that their children are more valuable than money. Therefore, mothers should stay at home with their children.

Passage 2

When people consider the subject of false or repressed memories, many seem to discount hypnosis as a plausible procedure. The media has printed numerous stories of the false accusations resulting from hypnosis.

In fact, hypnosis is a credible method of treatment in a variety of areas. Hypnosis can be used for medical treatment as a method of relaxation. Hypnotized patients learn to focus their attention on particular aspects of their environment and ignore the rest. Furthermore, psychologists also use hypnosis to treat neurotic symptoms, phobias, and memory problems.

The existence of one negative use of hypnosis has clouded the beneficial aspects of the procedure. Although a very few cases of false memories have arisen from hypnosis, it is still often a useful treatment procedure.

Passage 3

Alumni from Harvard, like the rest of us, are concerned about the risk of coronary heart disease. Together with cancer, these two complex diseases account for 70 percent of male deaths.

Researchers in a Palo Alto, California, sports medicine facility recently contacted Harvard alumni in an attempt to identify factors that might reduce coronary heart disease. They identified vigorous exercise as a critical factor in preventing death from this disease.

Several other research groups cautioned those who conducted the Harvard alumni study to be cautious about jumping to conclusions concerning the benefits of exercise. But after collecting data for several more years, the Palo Alto group concluded that vigorous exercise does indeed help prevent coronary heart disease.

Sample Responses

Passage 1

Because the author of the passage does not explicitly state a question, or issue, we must infer it by her conclusion and the concerns she raises throughout the passage. The first three paragraphs all mention problems that arise when mothers work outside the home. Both the indicator *therefore* and the location suggest that the final sentence of the fourth paragraph is the author's conclusion. Notice that this final sentence provides an answer to the issue just as a conclusion should do.

CONCLUSION: *Mothers should forgo work outside the home to care for their children.*

ISSUE: *Should mothers work outside the home?*

Passage 2

The first paragraph establishes the issue. It tells us what is on the writer's mind. The second sets the record straight from the perspective of the writer. The words *In fact* let you know that a conclusion is on the way. The third paragraph then indicates the rarity of the abuse of hypnosis. The point is that the negative effects of hypnosis are rare compared to the positive impacts.

CONCLUSION: *Yes, hypnosis is a beneficial procedure.*

ISSUE: *Should hypnosis be considered a useful psychological tool?*

Passage 3

Both indicator word and location clues aid us in finding the conclusion in this passage. The indicator word *concluded* is found in the last sentence.

CONCLUSION: *Vigorous exercise is a critical factor in preventing death from coronary heart disease.*

ISSUE: *Does vigorous physical activity help prevent death from coronary heart disease?*

Passage 4 (Self-Examination)

A recent court case in Hawaii involved the question of the legality of same-sex marriages. Because the majority of the United States is conservative, most people are probably against same-sex marriages. While most people consider the issue to be a clash of values, the question is really based on financial problems.

Same-sex couples face many financial problems that heterosexual couples do not face. For example, if a married person dies without a will, the property automatically transfers to the surviving spouse. However, same-sex couples must draft wills that leave their property to their partner. The cost of drafting these wills can range from $5,000 to $30,000. This cost is simply unfair to same-sex couples. Furthermore, health insurance for a heterosexual partner is usually offered through an employer. However, same-sex partners are not covered through employer insurance.

Although there are many financial biases against same-sex couples, these people face the problems because of their love for one another. In a country in which one out of every two new marriages ends in a divorce, we must not discriminate against those who practice love.

3

What Are the Reasons?

Reasons provide answers to our human curiosity about why someone makes a particular decision or holds a particular opinion.

> The legal drinking age should be 18.
>
> A pig is smarter than a mule.
>
> The sexual behavior of presidential candidates tells us something important about their fitness for office.
>
> Employers should be able to fire any employee who displeases them.

As information or advice, those four claims are missing something. We may or may not agree with them, but in their current form they neither strengthen nor weaken our initial positions. None of the claims contains an explanation or rationale for *why* we should agree. Thus, if we heard someone make one of those four assertions, we would be left hungry for more.

What is missing is the reason or reasons responsible for the claims. *Reasons* are beliefs, evidence, metaphors, analogies, and other statements offered to support or justify conclusions. They are the statements that together form the basis for demonstrating the credibility of a conclusion. Chapter 2 gave you some guidelines for locating two very important parts of the structure of an argument—the issue and the conclusion. This chapter focuses on techniques for identifying the third essential element of an argument—the reasons.

When a writer has a conclusion she wants you to accept, she must present reasons to persuade you that she is right, and to show you *why*.

It is the mark of a rational person to support his or her beliefs by adequate proof, especially when the beliefs are of a controversial nature. For example, when someone asserts that we should abolish the CIA, this assertion should be met with the challenge, "Why do you say that?" You should raise this question whether you agree or disagree. The person's reasons may be either strong or weak, but you will not know until you have asked the question and identified the reasons. If the answer is "because I think so," you should be dissatisfied with the argument, because the "reason" is a mere restatement of the conclusion. However, if the answer is evidence concerning wrongdoing by the CIA, you will want to consider such evidence when you evaluate the conclusion. *Remember:* You cannot determine the worth of a conclusion until you identify the reasons.

Identifying reasons is a particularly important step in critical thinking. An opinion cannot be evaluated fairly unless we ask why it is held and get a satisfactory response. Focusing on reasons requires us to remain open to and tolerant of views that might differ from our own. If we reacted to conclusions rather than to reasoning, we could tend to stick to the conclusions we brought to the discussion or essay, and those conclusions that agree with our own would receive our rapid assent. If we are ever to reexamine our own opinions, we must stay open to the reasons provided by those people with opinions that we do not yet share.

☞   *Critical Question:* **What are the reasons?**

Reasons + Conclusion = Argument

In ordinary conversation an argument refers to a disagreement, a time when blood pressure soars. We will use the concept in a slightly different manner. An *argument* is a combination of two forms of statements, a conclusion and the reasons allegedly supporting it. The partnership between reasons and conclusion establishes a person's argument.

Attention: Reasons are explanations or rationales for why we should believe a particular conclusion. They are what is offered as a basis for why we should accept the conclusion.

As we use the terms, *argument* and *reasoning* mean the same thing—the use of one or more ideas to support another idea. Thus when a communication lacks reasons, it is neither an argument nor an example of reasoning. Consequently, only arguments and reasoning can be logically flawed. Because a reason *by itself* is an isolated idea, it cannot reflect a logical relationship.

Several characteristics of arguments grab our attention:

- They have an intent. Those who provide them hope to convince us to believe certain things or act in certain ways. Consequently, they call for a reaction. We can imitate the sponge or the gold prospector, but we ordinarily must respond somehow.
- Their quality varies. Critical thinking is required to determine the degree of merit contained in an argument.
- They have two essential visible components—a conclusion and reasons. Failure to identify either component destroys the opportunity to evaluate the argument. We cannot evaluate what we cannot identify.

Initiating the Questioning Process

The first step in identifying reasons is to approach the argument with a questioning attitude, and the first question you should ask is a *why* question. You have identified the conclusion; now you wish to know why the conclusion makes sense. If a statement does not answer the question, "Why does the writer or speaker believe that?" then it is not a reason. In order to function as a reason, a statement (or group of statements) must provide support for a conclusion.

Let us apply the questioning attitude to the following paragraph. First we will find the conclusion; then we will ask the appropriate *why* question. Remember your guidelines for finding the conclusion. (The indicator words for the conclusion have been italicized.)

> (1) Is the cost of hospital care outrageous? (2) A recent survey by the American Association of Retired Persons offers reliable evidence on this issue. (3) Independent audits of the bills of 2,000 patients found that hospitals overcharge their patients by an average of 15 percent. (4) In addition, exit interviews with 400 patients revealed high amounts of dismay and anger when the patients were informed about the size of their total hospital bill. (5) *In short,* the costs of hospital care are higher than the services provided warrant.

What follows *In short* answers the question raised in statement (1). Thus, the conclusion is statement (5) ". . . the costs of hospital care are higher than the services provided warrant." *Highlight the conclusion!*

Attention: An argument consists of a conclusion and the reasons that allegedly support it.

We then ask the question, "Why does the writer or speaker believe the conclusion?" The statements that answer that question are the reasons. In this particular case, the writer provides us with evidence as reasons. Statements (3) and (4) jointly provide the evidence; that is, together they provide support for the conclusion. Together they serve as the reason for the conclusion. Thus, we can paraphrase the reason as: A survey shows that hospitals overcharge their patients and that patients are greatly dismayed about the size of their hospital bills.

Caution: A common misunderstanding at this point is to believe that a reason is not a reason if it is not very strong. If the writer or speaker believes that something is a reason, then at this stage of critical thinking, that something *is* a reason. Of course, we are moving rapidly in the direction of assessing the quality of reasons. But, at this stage, we are getting all the raw materials together in preparation for the assessment. So, use the communicator's intent as your guide as to whether something is a reason, at least for now.

DYNAMITE

Now, try to find the reasons in the following paragraph. Again, first find the conclusion, highlight it, and then ask the *why* question.

(1) Euthanasia is detrimental to the welfare of society because it destroys man's ideas of sacrifice, loyalty, and courage in bearing pain. (2) Some dying persons accept their suffering as a way of paying for their sins. (3) These people should be permitted to die as they wish—without help from any other person in speeding up the dying process.

There is no obvious indicator word for the conclusion in the paragraph, but the author is clearly arguing against the morality of euthanasia. The conclusion here is: "Euthanasia is detrimental to the welfare of society." Why does the author believe this? The major reason given is that "it destroys man's ideas of sacrifice, loyalty, and courage in bearing pain." The next two sentences in the excerpt provide additional support for this reason.

One of the best ways for you to determine whether you have discovered a reason is to try to play the role of the communicator. Put yourself in her position and ask yourself, "Why am I in favor of this conclusion that I am supporting?" Try to put into your own words how you believe the communicator would answer this question. If you can do this, you have probably discovered her reasons.

As you determine a communicator's reasoning structure, you should treat any idea that seems to be used to support his conclusion as a reason, even if you do not believe it provides support for the conclusion.

Words That Identify Reasons

As was the case with conclusions, there are certain words that will typically indicate that a reason will follow. *Remember:* The structure of reasoning is *this, because of that.* Thus, the word *because,* as well as words synonymous with and similar in function to it, will frequently signal the presence of reasons. A list of indicator words for reasons follows:

as a result of	for the reason that
because	in addition
since	in light of
first, . . . second	in view of the fact that
for	is supported by
for example	since the evidence is
for one thing	the study found that

Find the reasons in the following passage by identifying the indicator words.

(1) No one could be more willing to recommend hunting as a wholesome form of outdoor recreation than I. (2) For one thing, I believe that hunting has great value for those who participate in it. (3) It is a form of recreation that brings many physical, mental, and even spiritual benefits to the individual. (4) Hunting also develops self-reliance and confidence.

You should have identified statements (2) and (3) jointly as one reason, and (4) as another. Did you notice the indicator words *for one thing* and *also?*

Kinds of Reasons

There are many different kinds of reasons, depending on the kind of issue. Many reasons will be statements that present evidence. By *evidence,* we mean specific information that someone uses to furnish "proof" for something she is trying to claim is true. Communicators appeal to many kinds of evidence to "prove their point." These include "the facts," research findings, examples from real life, statistics, appeals to experts and authorities, personal testimonials, metaphors, and analogies. Different kinds of evidence are more appropriate in some situations than in others, and you will find it helpful to develop rules for yourself for determining what kinds of evidence are appropriate on given occasions.

You will often want to ask, "What kind of evidence is needed to support this claim?" and then determine whether such evidence has been offered. You should know that there are no uniform "codes of evidence" applicable to all cases of serious reasoning. A more detailed treatment of evidence appears in Chapters 8–11.

When a speaker or writer is trying to support a descriptive conclusion, the answer to the *why* question will typically be evidence.

The following example provides a descriptive argument; try to find the author's reasons.

> (1) The fact is that college women are now smoking cigarettes at an increasing rate. (2) Recent surveys show that as male college students have decreased their consumption by 40 percent, females have increased their consumption of cigarettes by 60 percent.

You should have identified the first statement as the conclusion. It is a descriptive statement about the rate at which women in college are smoking cigarettes. The rest of the paragraph presents the evidence—the reason for the conclusion. *Remember:* The conclusion itself will not be evidence; it will be a belief supported by evidence or by other beliefs.

In prescriptive arguments, reasons are typically either general, prescriptive statements, or they are descriptive statements. The use of these kinds of statements to support a conclusion in a prescriptive argument is illustrated in the following:

> (1) With regard to the big controversy over grade inflation, I would like to ask a few questions. (2) What difference does it make if the people who are really good are never distinguished from the average student? (3) Is there a caste system in our society according to grade-point averages?
>
> (4) Are those with high grade-point averages superior to those with low grade-point averages? (5) In the majority of cases, grades are not a true indication of learning, anyway; they are a measure of how well a student can absorb information for a short time period and regurgitate it on a test.
>
> (6) Students will retain the information that interests them and is important anyway. (7) Why can't we eliminate grades and be motivated only by the inborn curiosity and zest for learning that is really in us all?

The controversy here is what to do about grade inflation. The author's solution to the problem is to abolish grades, as indicated in sentence (7). Let's look for sentences that answer the question, "Why does the author believe this conclusion?" First, note that no evidence is presented. Sentences (2) and (3) jointly form one reason: It is not important to distinguish the average student from the good student. Note that this is a general principle that indicates the writer's view about how the world should be. Sentences (4) and (5) add a second reason: Grades are not a true indicator of learning. This is a general belief regarding a disadvantage of grades. Sentence (6) provides a third reason: Students will retain only the information that interests them and is important anyway (grades do not help learners to remember). This is another general belief. The beliefs themselves may be supported by evidence in some form.

Keeping the Reasons and Conclusions Straight

As you read critically, the reasons and the conclusions are the most important elements to bring into clear focus. Much reasoning is long and not very well organized. Sometimes a set of reasons will support one conclusion, and that conclusion will function as the main reason for another conclusion. Reasons may be supported by other reasons. In especially complicated arguments, it is frequently difficult to keep the structure straight in your mind as you attempt to critically evaluate what you have read. To overcome this problem, try to develop your own organizing procedure for keeping the reasons and conclusions separate and in a logical pattern.

Some readers have found the following suggestions useful:

1. Circle indicator words.
2. Underline the reasons and conclusion in different colors of ink, or highlight the conclusion and underline the reasons.
3. Label the reasons and conclusion in the margin.
4. After reading long passages, make a list of reasons at the end of the essay.
5. For especially complicated reasoning, diagram the structure, using numbers to refer to each reason and conclusion and arrows to designate the direction of their relationships. Sometimes this technique is most effective if all reasons and conclusions are first paraphrased in the margins, then numbered.

We can illustrate these suggested techniques by attempting to find the conclusion and reasons in the following relatively complex passage.

(1) Do physicians have a moral obligation to provide free medical care for those who cannot pay? (2) *Yes, they do.* (3) *First,* society has restricted most medical practice to physicians, resulting in a medical monopoly that has obvious benefits. (4) *Thus, it seems reasonable that* the profession acknowledge its collective responsibility to provide care even to those who cannot pay.

(5) *Second,* the moral obligation of individual physicians to provide free care derives from an understanding of their special role. (6) Physicians should not be compared to plumbers or car mechanics, or to other craftsmen who repair inanimate objects. (7) Unlike automobile repairs, the health problems of people are not deferrable or negotiable. (8) That doctors help some people without pay is essential if doctors are to remain doctors and medical services are not to be regarded as just another form of profit-seeking business activity.[1]

Initially you should notice that we have italicized the conclusion and key indicator words. As you read this passage, you surely noticed that the reasoning structure is quite complicated. For such a passage, we have to understand the

[1]Adapted from M. Siegler, "Treating the Jobless for Free: Do Doctors Have a Special Duty? Yes," *The Hastings Center Report* (August 1983), 12–13.

logical sequence of sentences to isolate the reasoning structure. Thus we have diagrammed the relationships among the reasons and conclusion. Try to diagram this passage on your own; then, compare your diagram to ours.

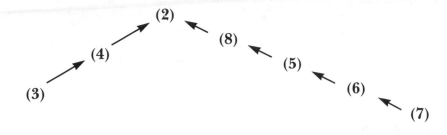

Our diagram reflects our interpretation that sentence (4) in paragraph 1 and sentence (8) in paragraph 2 directly answered the question, "Why is the conclusion, sentence (2), true?" The direction of the rest of the arrows in the diagram denotes how we believe these two reasons are supported by further reasons. For example, statement (6) provides support for (5).

Diagramming is useful for gaining an understanding of especially complicated arguments. When reading lengthy essays, it is always useful to paraphrase the main reasons in the margins. Thus, for the above passage, we might have supplied the following paraphrased reasons:

Paragraph 1: Physicians owe a debt to society.

Paragraph 2: The physician's role is special; physicians are unlike businessmen.

We have mentioned a number of techniques for you to use in developing a clear picture of the reasoning structure. If some other technique works better for you, by all means use it. The important point is to keep the reasons and conclusions straight as you prepare to evaluate.

Reasons First, Then Conclusions

The first chapter warned you about the danger of weak-sense critical thinking. A warning signal that can alert you to weak-sense critical thinking should go off when you notice that reasons seem to be created (on the spot, even) only because they defend a previously held opinion. When someone is eager to share an opinion as if it were a conclusion, but looks puzzled or angry when asked for reasons, weak-sense critical thinking is the probable culprit.

Certainly, you have a large set of initial beliefs, which act as initial conclusions when you encounter controversies. As your respect for the importance of reasons grows, you will frequently expect those conclusions to stand or crumble on the basis of their support. Your strongest conclusions follow your reflection about the reasons and what they mean.

Be your own censor in this regard. You must shake your own pan when looking for gold. Try to avoid "reverse logic" or "backward reasoning," whereby reasons are an afterthought, following the selection of your conclusion. Ideally, reasons are the tool by which conclusions are shaped and modified.

"Fresh" Reasons and Your Growth

We need to remind ourselves again and again how important it is to force ourselves to pay attention to "fresh" reasons, those that we have not previously considered. Being fair to such reasons is tough, but rewarding. What makes this task so difficult is our current opinions. They provide a starting point for our reaction to reasoning. We come to each conversation, essay, or lecture with a loyalty to the beliefs we already have. Thus our existing beliefs can be an obstacle to our listening and learning. But at another level we know there are thoughtful reasons that we have not yet encountered. For our personal growth we have to give "fresh" reasons a real chance to speak to us.

Reasons and Effective Writing

When you are writing, you will usually want to make your reader's job as easy as possible. Thus, your task is to use words, sentences, paragraphs, and indicator words to illuminate the logical relationships in your argument.

A good way to begin is by clearly outlining or diagramming your reasoning structure. Then keep several fundamental rules in mind as you write. The first is the rule of *grouping:* Keep reasons for the same conclusion together. You can do this by keeping grammatical structure parallel and by using appropriate indicator words. The second is the rule of *direction.* After you have developed a sequential order of reasons, such that each reason relates to a subsequent one, word your essay so that the reasons move in a single direction. For example, a sequence that follows the rule of direction goes from the final conclusion to its main reason to the reason for that reason.

A third rule is that of keeping reasons that bear a similar relationship to the conclusion in close proximity to one another, so that their relationship is easy to see. Do not separate them with reasons that involve quite different considerations.

Practice Exercises

☞ *Critical Question:* **What are the reasons?**

First survey the passage and highlight its conclusion. Then ask the question, why? and locate the reasons. Use indicator words to help. Keep the conclusions and the reasons separate.

Passage 1

Divorce is on the increase, and we're worried. Finally, psychologists have identified a key cause of divorce. Noticing that certain families have multiple divorces, they found that inherited genes play a major role in causing divorces.

Although the overall divorce rate is 20 percent, psychologists discovered that a twin has a 45 percent rate of divorce *if* the identical twin has already experienced a divorce. Additional confirming evidence for genes as a primary cause stems from looking at the divorce rate of twins' parents. If these parents have divorced, each twin has a 10 percent higher risk of divorce.

Passage 2

Eunice Kennedy Shriver stood up for parents on the Op-Ed page of *The Washington Post* recently. In a piece entitled, "Yes, Parents Should Know," she supported the Health and Human Services Department's proposed rule to require that federally funded family-planning clinics notify the parents of minors to whom they are providing prescription contraceptives.

Mrs. Shriver's arguments for the proposed rule, which echo the administration's, reveal much well-meaning intent and a distorted view of reality. Mandatory notification is more likely to deter girls from using the clinic than to benefit girls who come home to find their parents reading a government notice announcing that their daughter has obtained birth control.

The premise behind mandatory notification is that adolescent knowledge of human sexuality causes adolescent promiscuity. No evidence has yet been offered that can support this premise. Indeed, the June report by the Alan Guttmaker Institute found that sex education in schools does not promote promiscuity in teenagers, and may even discourage teenage pregnancy. Planned Parenthood does not introduce teenagers to sex; girls who come to this clinic have been having sex for an average of nine months before their first visit.[2]

Passage 3

Speedy, colorful waterscooters are gaining in popularity. Waterscooters can travel anywhere a small boat can and are typically popular with young people. The rising popularity of the craft has raised the question of waterscooter regulation. In this case, the argument for strict regulation is compelling. Waterscooters are a particularly deadly form of water recreation.

For example, two women were vacationing in Longboat Key. While they were floating on a raft along the shore, a waterscooter crashed into them and killed them. Also, waterscooter operators have been killed or seriously injured in collisions with other water craft. Others have been stranded at sea when their scooters either failed or sank far from shore. Many waterscooter operators are inexperienced and ignorant of navigational rules, increasing the potential for accidents. The increasing popularity of the scooter has exacerbated the problem, providing more water vehicles to compete for the same space. Crowded waterways are simply an open invitation to disaster.

[2]Adapted from A. Shlaes, "The Squeal Squawk," *The New Republic* (August 9, 1982), 18–20.

In addition to the inherent operational hazards of waterscooters, they are proving to be an environmental nuisance. Beach residents complain of the intrusive noise of the scooters. The Pacific Whale Foundation on the West Coast expressed concern that the scooters are frightening away endangered humpback whales that migrate to Hawaii for breeding.

Regulations stipulating minimum operating age, restricted operating areas, and mandatory classes in water safety are essential. Without such regulations, tragedies involving waterscooters are sure to multiply, rendering many beaches unsafe for recreation.

Sample Responses

Passage 1

ISSUE: *What causes divorce?*

CONCLUSION: *Inherited genes explain who is at greatest risk of divorce.*

REASONS: 1. *A twin whose twin has divorced a spouse has much greater than normal risk of also experiencing divorce.*
2. *When a twin's parents are divorced, the twin's risk of divorce shoots up by 10 percent.*

Recall that we are looking for the support system for the conclusion. We ask ourselves: Why does this person claim that genes play a major role in causing divorces? The conclusion is justified because psychologists "found that. . . ." This finding provides the first reason. The second is discovered when we see that "additional confirming evidence" exists. That evidence provides the second reason.

Passage 2

ISSUE: *Should federally funded family-planning clinics be required to notify the parents of minors to whom they are providing prescription contraceptives?*

CONCLUSION: *No, they should not be required to do so.*

REASONS: 1. *The rule is likely to deter girls from using the clinic.*
2. *Knowledge of human sexuality does not cause adolescent promiscuity. This claim is supported by findings from the Guttmaker Institute.*

What is it that is supposed to make us accept the view of that federally funded clinics should not be required to notify the parents of minors to whom they are providing prescription contraceptives? The first reason comes to us by way of the author's statement that such a rule will have a different effect than proponents suggest. Instead of helping these young women, such a rule will play a role in preventing them from even coming to the clinic.

The second reason appears when we see the reference to a study done by a research institute. So this reason is in the form: this study shows that. . . .

Passage 3

ISSUE: *Should waterscooters be subject to strict regulation?*

CONCLUSION: *Yes, waterscooters should be strictly regulated.*

REASONS: *1. Waterscooters are extremely dangerous.*
  a. Operators are killing themselves and others.
  b. Most waterscooter operators are inexperienced.
  c. The growing popularity of the scooters has resulted in crowding, worsening the problem.
  2. Waterscooters pose an environmental threat.

Why are we told that waterscooters should be strictly regulated? The answer to that question will be the author's reasons. The first reason is a collection of examples and claims, all trying to make us aware of the extreme danger faced by those who dare to get on the waterscooters. *In addition* are the indicator words that call our attention to the second of the two reasons. That reason is the environmental hazard created by the unregulated use of the waterscooters.

Passage 4 (Self-Examination)

I really believe that the legal age for drinking alcohol should be lowered to 18. The evidence is overwhelming that those who reach the age of 18 are responsible adults. For instance, they are allowed to vote and sign legally binding contracts at that age. Surely the adults who granted those rights and responsibilities to those of us who reach 18 know we are responsible enough to handle them.

For one thing, we witness all around us the misuse of alcohol by those much older than 18. We can learn from their mistakes and avoid the pain they have experienced from alcohol abuse. We don't want to hurt ourselves or anyone else. We will be careful.

Also, I can buy tobacco when I am 18. Studies have shown us that tobacco causes even more deaths than alcohol does. As long as tobacco can be bought at 18, setting the legal age for alcohol at 21 is not going to put a stop to premature death. Let's face it: when we reach 18 we deserve the right to demonstrate that we have learned more in school than just how to read and write. In light of the years and years that we have been in classes where we have been taught responsibility, we are ready to use alcohol in a responsible fashion.

4

What Words
or Phrases Are Ambiguous?

The first three chapters of this book help you identify the basic structural elements in any message. At this point, if you can locate a writer's or speaker's conclusion and reasons, you are progressing rapidly toward the ultimate goal of forming your own rational decisions. Your next step is to put this structural picture into clearer focus.

While identifying the conclusion and reasons gives you the basic visible structure, you still need to examine the precise *meaning* of these parts before you can react fairly to the ideas being presented. You need now to pay much more attention to the details of the language.

Deciding on the precise meaning of key words or phrases is an essential prerequisite to deciding whether to agree with someone's opinion. If you fail to check for the meaning of crucial terms and phrases, you may react to an opinion the author never intended.

Let's see why knowing the meaning of a communicator's terms is so important.

Recently, in Michigan, a lawyer filed charges against a psychologist, accusing him of failing to report a teenaged girl's allegations that her stepfather had sexually abused her. The prosecution argued that the psychologist's continued treatment of the father and stepdaughter indicated that he had *reasonable cause to suspect* the abuse occurred.

We hope that you can see that judging whether the psychologist made a bad decision rests on the meaning of *reasonable cause to suspect;* yet, this phrase has many different possible meanings. If you were a juror, wouldn't you want to know the meaning of this phrase before deciding whether the psychologist was guilty? If you would, you would be agreeing with the defense lawyer who argued that the phrase *reasonable cause to suspect* is subjective and too vague, unless clarified.

This courtroom example illustrates an important point: You cannot react to an argument unless you understand the meanings (explicit or implied) of crucial terms and phrases. How these are interpreted will often affect the acceptability of the reasoning. Consequently, before you can determine the extent to which you wish to accept one conclusion or another, you must first attempt to discover the precise meaning of the conclusion and the reasons. While their meaning typically *appears* obvious, it often is not.

The discovery and clarification of meaning require conscious, step-by-step procedures. This chapter suggests one set of such procedures. If focuses on the following question:

☞   *Critical Question:* **What words or phrases are ambiguous?**

The Confusing Flexibility of Words

Our language is highly complex. If each word had only one potential meaning about which we all agreed, effective communication would be more likely. However, most words have more than one meaning.

Consider the multiple meanings of such words as *freedom, obscenity,* and *happiness.* These multiple meanings can create serious problems in determining the worth of an argument. For example, when someone argues that a magazine should not be published because it is obscene, you cannot evaluate the argument until you know what the writer means by *obscene.* In this brief argument, it is easy to find the conclusion and the supporting reason, but the quality of the reasoning is difficult to judge because of the ambiguous use of *obscene.* Thus, even when you can identify the structure of what others are saying, you still must struggle with the meaning of certain words in that structure. A warning: *We often misunderstand what we read because we presume that what words mean is obvious.*

Whenever you are reading or listening, force yourself to *search for ambiguity;* otherwise, you may simply miss the point. A term or phrase is ambiguous when its meaning is so uncertain in the context of the discourse we are examining that we need further clarification before we can judge the adequacy of the reasoning.

As a further illustration of potential problems caused by not making the meaning of terms sufficiently clear, look at the following argument; then write out the "obvious" meaning of the term *social worth.*

> More and more of us are being kept alive for extended periods of time by medical wizardry. This development is causing a strain on pension plans and social security. Unfortunately, our economy seems unable to meet both the expensive needs of the aged and the resource claims made by every other group in society. Hence, I wish to propose that we change our attitude toward the ultimate desirability of a long life. Instead, we should think in terms of the quality of life. At any point in a person's life at which his or her social worth has become minimal, we should relax our fear of suicide. Those adults who choose to escape the potential misery of old age should be permitted to do so without the rebuke of those who survive them.

How did you do? What the author is suggesting isn't clear at all, because we don't know whether he thinks that *social worth* means (1) the economic contribution that a person can make, *or* (2) the benefits of human communication and interaction. Does it really matter which of these possible interpretations the author means? It certainly does. The argument would be more persuasive if the writer meant the second definition. If he intended the first definition, then he is advocating a major social change based on a very narrow concept of what it means to be human. Notice that the clues about the meaning of the term are sketchy at best. Until we find out that meaning, we aren't well prepared to form a reaction to the argument.

Locating Key Terms and Phrases

The first step in determining which terms or phrases are ambiguous is to use the stated issue as a clue for possible key terms. Key terms or phrases will be those terms that may have more than one plausible meaning within the context of the issue; that is, terms that you know any communicator addressing this issue will have to make clear before you can decide to agree or disagree with her. To illustrate the potential benefit of checking terminology in the issue, let's examine several stated issues:

1. Does TV violence adversely affect society?
2. Is the Miss America contest demeaning to women?
3. Is the incidence of rape in our society increasing?

Attention: Ambiguity refers to the existence of multiple possible meanings for a word or phrase.

Each of these stated issues contains phrases that writers or speakers will have to make clear before you will be able to evaluate their response to the issue. Each of the following phrases is potentially ambiguous: TV violence, adversely affect society, demeaning to women, and incidence of rape. Thus, when you read an essay responding to these issues, you will want to pay close attention to how the author has defined these terms.

The next step in determining which terms or phrases are ambiguous is to identify what words or phrases seem crucial in determining how well the author's reasons support his conclusion, that is, to identify the *key terms in the reasoning structure.* Once you do that, you can then determine whether the meaning of these terms is ambiguous.

When searching for key terms and phrases, you should keep in mind *why* you are looking. Someone wants you to accept a conclusion. Therefore, you are looking only for those terms or phrases that will affect whether you accept the conclusion. *So, look for them in the reasons and conclusion.* Terms and phrases that are not included in the basic reasoning structure can thus be "dumped from your pan"; you only want to think hard about the meaning of terms in the reasons and conclusion.

Another useful guide for searching for key terms and phrases is to keep in mind the following rule: The more abstract a word or phrase, the more likely it is to be susceptible to multiple interpretations and thus need clear definition by the author. To avoid being unclear in our use of the term *abstract*, we define it here in the following way: A term becomes more and more abstract as it refers less and less to particular, specific instances. Thus, the words *equality, responsibility, pornography,* and *aggression* are much more abstract than are the phrases "having equal access to necessities of life," "directly causing an event," "pictures of male and female genitals," and "doing deliberate physical harm to another person." These phrases provide a much more concrete picture and are therefore less ambiguous.

You can also locate potential important ambiguous phrases by *reverse role playing.* That is, ask yourself, if you were to *adopt a position contrary to the author's,* would you choose to define certain terms or phrases differently? If so, you have identified a possible ambiguity. For example, someone who sees beauty pageants as desirable is likely to define "demeaning to women" quite differently from someone who sees them as undesirable.

Checking for Ambiguity

You now know where to look for those terms or phrases that are ambiguous. The next step is to focus on each term or phrase and ask yourself, "Do I understand its meaning?" In answering this very important question, you will need to overcome several major obstacles.

One obstacle is assuming that you and the author mean the same thing. Thus, you need to begin your search by avoiding "mind-reading." You need to get into the habit of asking, "What do you mean by that?" instead of, "I know just what you mean." A second obstacle is assuming that terms have a single, obvious definition. Many terms do not. Thus, always ask, "Could any of the words or phrases have a different meaning?"

You can be certain you have identified an especially important unclear term by performing the following test. If you can express two or more alternative meanings for a term, each of which makes sense in the context of the argument, and if the extent to which a reason would support a conclusion is affected by which meaning is assumed, then you have located a significant ambiguity. Thus, a good test for determining whether you have identified an important ambiguity is to *substitute* the alternative meanings into the reasoning structure and see whether changing the meaning *makes a difference* in how well a reason supports the conclusion.

Caution: The previous paragraph would be put in fluorescent lights if this book were in multimedia mode. What it does is provide you with a format for both checking yourself and convincing others that you have indeed discovered an ambiguity that needs pursuing. Without some approach like the one described above, it is too easy to think that this part of critical thinking has been completed just because you think that you have found a word or phrase with multiple meanings. What you are looking for, instead, is a particular kind of ambiguity—one that jolts the reasoning in one direction or another, depending on which meaning of the ambiguous term or phrase is assumed.

DYNAMITE

Determining Ambiguity

Let's now apply the above hints in determining which key terms a communicator has not made sufficiently clear. Remember: As we do this exercise, keep asking, "What does the author mean by that?" and pay particular attention to abstract terms.

We will start with a simple reasoning structure: an advertisement.

Lucky Smokes put it all together and got taste with only 3 mg. tar.

ISSUE: *What cigarette should you buy?*

CONCLUSION: (implied): *Buy Lucky Smokes.*

REASON: *They got taste with only 3 mg. tar.*

The phrases "Buy Lucky Smokes" and "3 mg. tar" seem quite concrete and self-evident. But, how about "got taste?" Is the meaning obvious? We think not. How do we know? Let's perform a test together. Could taste have more than one meaning? Yes. It could mean a barely noticeable mild tobacco flavor. It could mean a rather harsh, bitter flavor. Or it could have many other meanings. Isn't it true that you would be more eager to follow the advice of the advertisement if the taste provided matched your taste preference? Thus, the ambiguity is significant because it affects the degree to which you might be persuaded by the ad.

Advertising is often full of ambiguity. Advertisers intentionally engage in ambiguity to persuade you that their products are superior to those of their competitors. They want you to choose the meaning of ambiguous terms that is personally more desirable. Here are some sample advertising claims that are ambiguous. See if you can identify alternative, plausible meanings for the italicized words or phrases.

> No-Pain is the *extra-strength* pain reliever.
>
> Parvu: Sensual . . . but not *too far from innocence.*
>
> Ray Rhinestone's new album: an album of *experiences.*
>
> Vital Hair Vitamins show you *what* vitamins can do for your hair.
>
> Here is a book at last that shows you how to find and keep a *good man.*

In each case, the advertiser hoped that you would assign the most attractive meaning to the ambiguous words. Critical reading can sometimes protect you from making purchasing decisions that you would later regret.

Let's now look at a more complicated example of ambiguity. Remember to begin by identifying the issue, conclusion, and reasons.

> It is time to take active steps in reducing the amount of violence on television. The adverse effect of such violence is clear, as evidenced by many recent research studies. Several studies indicate that heavy TV watchers tend to overestimate the danger of physical violence in real life. Other studies show that children who are heavy TV watchers can become desensitized to violence in the real world. Numerous other studies demonstrate the adverse effect of TV violence.

This essay addresses the issue, should we do something about the violence on television? It concludes that we ought to take active steps to reduce the amount of TV violence, and the author's main reason supporting the conclusion is that such violence has an adverse effect. The writer then uses research evidence to support this reasoning. Let's examine the reasoning for any words or phrases that would affect our willingness to accept it.

First, let's examine the issue for terms we will want the author to make clear. Certainly, we would not be able to agree or disagree with this author's conclusion until she has indicated what she means by "violence on television." Thus, we will want to check how clearly she has defined it in her reasoning.

Next, let's list all key terms and phrases in the conclusion and reasons: "take active steps in reducing the amount of violence on television," "adverse effect," "many recent research studies," "several studies," "heavy TV watchers," "tend to overestimate the danger of physical violence in real life," "other studies," "children who are heavy TV watchers," "can become desensitized to violence in the real world," "numerous other studies," "demonstrate," "adverse effect of TV violence." Let's take a close look at a few of these to determine whether they could have different meanings that might make a difference in how we would react to the reasoning.

First, her conclusion is ambiguous. Exactly what does it mean to "take active steps in reducing the amount of violence?" Does it mean to impose a legal ban against showing any act of physical violence, or might it mean putting public pressure on the networks to restrict violent episodes to late evening hours? Before you could decide whether to agree with the speaker or writer, you would first have to decide what it is she wants us to believe.

Next, she argues that "heavy" TV watchers "overestimate the danger of physical violence in real life" and "become desensitized to violence in the real world." But how much TV does one have to watch to qualify as a heavy TV watcher? Perhaps most people are not heavy TV watchers, given the actual research study's definition of that phrase. Also, what does it mean to overestimate the danger of physical violence, or to become desensitized? Try to create a mental picture of what these phrases represent. If you can't, the phrases are ambiguous.

Now, check the other phrases we listed above. Do they not also need to be clarified? You can see that if you accept this writer's argument without requiring her to clarify these ambiguous phrases, you will not have understood what it is you agreed to believe.

Context and Ambiguity

Writers and speakers only rarely define their terms. Thus, typically your only guide to the meaning of an ambiguous statement is the *context* in which the words are used. By *context*, we mean the writer's or speaker's background, traditional use of the term within the particular controversy, and the words and statements preceding and following the possible ambiguity. All three elements provide clues to the meaning of a potential key term or phrase.

If you were to see the term *human rights* in an essay, you should immediately ask yourself, "What rights are those?" If you examine the context and find that the writer is a leading member of the Norwegian government, it is a good bet that the human rights he has in mind are the rights to be employed, receive free health care, and obtain adequate housing. An American senator might mean something very different by human rights. She could have in mind freedoms of speech, religion, travel, and peaceful assembly. Notice that the two versions of human rights are not necessarily consistent. A country could guarantee one form of human rights and at the same time violate the other. You must try to clarify such terms by examining their context.

Writers frequently make clear their assumed meaning of a term by their arguments. The following paragraph is an example:

> Studies show that most people who undergo psychotherapy benefit from the experience. In fact, a recent study shows that after ten sessions of psychotherapy, two-thirds of participants reported experiencing less anxiety.

The phrase "benefit from the experience" is potentially ambiguous, because it could have a variety of meanings. However, the writer's argument makes clear that *in this context,* "benefit from the experience" means reporting less anxiety.

Note that, even in this case, you would want some further clarification before you call a therapist, because "reporting less anxiety" is ambiguous. Wouldn't you want to know how *much* lowering of anxiety was experienced? Perhaps participants still experienced significant amounts of anxiety—but less than previously.

A major advantage of recognizing that terms or phrases may have multiple meanings is that locating the author's meaning offers the option of *disagreeing* with it. If you disagree with a debatable, assumed definition, then you will want to recognize that the quality of the author's reasoning is conditional upon the definition used, and you will not want to be unduly influenced by the reasoning. Thus, in the above example you may believe that a preferred definition of "benefits of psychotherapy" is "a major restructuring of personality characteristics." If so, *for you,* the author's reason would not be supportive of the conclusion.

Examine the context carefully to determine the meaning of key terms and phrases. If the meaning remains uncertain, you have located an important ambiguity. If the meaning is clear and you disagree with it, then you should be wary of any reasoning that involves that term or phrase.

Ambiguity, Definitions, and the Dictionary

It should be obvious from the preceding discussion that to locate and clarify ambiguity, you must be aware of the possible meanings of words. Meanings usually come in one of three forms: synonyms, examples, and what we will call "definition by specific criteria." For example, one could offer at least three different definitions of *anxiety:*

1. Anxiety is feeling nervous. (*synonym*)
2. Anxiety is what Bill Clinton experienced when he turned on the television to watch the election returns. (*example*)
3. Anxiety is a subjective feeling of discomfort accompanied by increased sensitivity of the autonomic nervous system. (*specific criteria*)

For critical evaluation of most controversial issues, synonyms and examples are inadequate. They fail to tell you the specific properties that are crucial for an unambiguous understanding of the term. Useful definitions are those that specify criteria for usage—and the more specific the better.

Where do you go for your definitions? One obvious and very important source is your dictionary. However, dictionary definitions frequently consist of synonyms, examples, or incomplete specifications of criteria for usage. These definitions often do not adequately define the use of a term in a particular essay. In such cases, you must discover possible meanings from the context of the passage, or from what else you know about the topic. We suggest you keep a dictionary handy, but keep in mind that the appropriate definition may not be there.

Let's take a closer look at some of the inadequacies of a dictionary definition. Examine the following brief paragraph.

> Education is not declining in quality at this university. In my interviews, I found that an overwhelming majority of the students and instructors responded that they saw no decline in the quality of education here.

It is clearly important to know what is meant by "quality of education" in the above paragraph. If you look up the word *quality* in the dictionary, you will find many meanings, the most appropriate, given this context, being *excellence* or *superiority*. *Excellence* and *superiority* are synonyms for *quality*—and they are equally abstract. You still need to know precisely what is meant by *excellence* or *superiority*. How do you know whether education is high in quality or excellence? Ideally, you would want the writer to tell you precisely what *behaviors* he is referring to when he uses the phrase "quality of education." Can you think of some different ways that the phrase might be defined? The following list presents some possible definitions of *quality of education:*

average grade-point average of students

ability of students to think critically

number of professors who have doctoral degrees

amount of work usually required to pass an exam

Each of these definitions suggests a different way to measure quality; each specifies a different criterion. Each provides a concrete way in which the term could be used. Note also that each of these definitions will affect the degree to which you will want to agree with the author's reasoning. For example, if you believe that "quality" should refer to the ability of students to think critically, and most of the students in the interviews are defining it as how much work is required for you to pass an exam, the reason would not *necessarily* support the conclusion. Exams may not require the ability to think critically.

Thus, in many arguments you will not be able to find adequate dictionary definitions, and the context may not make the meaning clear. One way to discover possible alternative meanings is to try to create a mental picture of what the words represent. If you cannot do so, then you probably have identified an important ambiguity. Let's apply such a test to the following example:

> Welfare programs have not succeeded. They have not provided the poor with productive jobs.

The provision of productive jobs for the poor is the standard being used here to assess the worth of welfare programs. Can you create a single clear mental picture of *productive jobs?* Are there alternative definitions? Does *productive* mean "leading to greater profit" or "providing a sense of self-worth?" If you wanted to check on the accuracy of the reasoning, wouldn't you first need to know when a job is productive? You cannot count those jobs that are productive until the meaning of *productive jobs* is clarified. Thus, we have located an important ambiguity.

Caution: This section contains the first formal critical thinking tool. Specifically, point out to yourself and to others that you cannot accept reasoning that is so incomplete that you would not understand what you are accepting. If we think of critical thinking as the application of rational standards to reasoning, a person who leaves us with ambiguous reasoning has violated one of those standards. While we want to give the communicator a full opportunity to clarify the ambiguity, if he or she is unable or unwilling to do so, our response as critical thinkers must be:

Well then, I cannot accept your argument.

DYNAMITE

Ambiguity and Loaded Language

Ambiguity is not always an accident. Those trying to persuade you are often quite aware that words have multiple meanings. Furthermore, they know that certain of those meanings carry with them heavy emotional baggage. Words like *sacrifice* and *justice* have multiple meanings, and some of those meanings are loaded in the sense that they stimulate certain emotions in us. Anyone trying to use language to lead us by the heart can take advantage of these probable emotions.

Political language is often loaded *and* ambiguous. For example, *welfare* is often how we refer to governmental help to those we don't like; when help from the government goes to groups we like, we call it *a subsidy* or *an incentive.* The following table consists of political terms and the intended emotional impact.

Ambiguous Political Language	
Term	**Emotional Impact**
Revenue Enhancement	Positive response to tax hikes
Tax and Spend Democrats	Irresponsible and wasteful
Restoring Fairness	Approval of proposed tax changes
Extreme	Undesirable, unreasonable
Terrorist	Wild, crazy, uncivilized
Defense spending	Needed, protective, required
Reform	Desirable changes

All the terms in the table are ambiguous. As critical thinkers, we must be sensitive to the intended emotional impact and the role of ambiguity in encouraging that impact. By searching for alternative meanings of terms such as *reform*, we can safeguard ourselves against easy emotional commitments to arguments we would otherwise question. After all, even the most dangerous political change is in some sense a "reform."

Norman Solomon's *The Power of Babble* provides a colorful illustration of how successful politicians use ambiguous language to persuade others. Note that Mr. Solomon has conveniently placed key ambiguous terms in alphabetical order for us.

America is back, and bipartisan—biting the bullet with competitiveness, diplomacy, efficiency, empowerment, end games, and environmentalism, along with faith in the founding Fathers, freedom's blessings, free markets and free peoples, and most of all, God. Our great heritage has held the line for human rights, individual initiative, justice, kids, leadership, liberty, loyalty, mainstream values, the marketplace, measured responses, melting pots, the middle class, military reform, moderates, modernization, moral standards, national security, and Old Glory. Opportunity comes from optimism, patriotism, peace through strength, the people, pluralism, and points of light. Pragmatism and the power of prayer make for principle while the private sector protects the public interest. Realism can mean recycling, self-discipline, and the spirit of '76, bring stability and standing tall for strategic interests and streamlined taxation. Uncle Sam has been undaunted ever since Valley Forge, with values venerated by veterans; vigilance, vigor, vision, voluntarism, and Western values.

Limits of Your Responsibility to Clarify Ambiguity

After you have attempted to identify and clarify ambiguity, what can you do if you are still uncertain about the meaning of certain key ideas? What is a reasonable next step? We suggest you ignore any reason containing ambiguity that makes it impossible to judge the acceptability of the reason. It is your responsibility as an active learner to ask questions that clarify ambiguity. However, your responsibility stops at that point. It is the writer or speaker who is trying to convince you of something. Her role as a persuader requires her to respond to your concerns about possible ambiguity.

You are not required to react to ideas or options that are unclear. If a friend tells you that you should enroll in a class because it "really is different," but cannot tell you how it is different, then you have no basis for agreeing or disagreeing with the advice. No one has the right to be believed if he cannot provide you with a clear picture of his reasoning.

Ambiguity and Effective Writing

Although most of this chapter is addressed to you as a critical reader, it is also extremely relevant to improved writing. Effective writers strive for clarity. They review their writing several times, looking for any statements that might be ambiguous.

Look back at the section on "Locating Key Terms and Phrases." Use the hints given there for finding important ambiguity to revise your own writing. For instance, abstractions that are ambiguous can be clarified by concrete illustrations, conveying the meaning you intend. Pay special attention to the reason and conclusion in any essay you write; ambiguity can be an especially serious problem in those elements.

Thinking about the characteristics of your intended audience can help you decide where ambiguities need to be clarified. Jargon or specific abstractions that would be very ambiguous to a general audience may be adequately understood by a specialized audience. Remember that the reader will probably not struggle for a long time with your meaning. If you confuse your reader, you will probably lose her quickly. If you never regain her attention, then you have failed in your task as a writer.

Summary

You cannot evaluate an essay until you know the communicator's intended meaning of key terms and phrases as well as alternative meanings they could conceivably have had in the context of the argument. You can find important clues to potential ambiguity in the statement of the issue and can locate key words and phrases in the reasons and confusions. Because many authors fail to define their terms and because many key terms have multiple meanings, you must search for possible ambiguity. You do this by asking the questions, "What *could* be meant?" and "What *is* meant by the key terms? Once you have completed the search, you will know four very important components of the reasoning:

1. the key terms and phrases,
2. which of these are adequately defined,
3. which of these possess other possible definitions, which if substituted, would modify your reaction to the reasoning, and
4. which of these are ambiguous within the context of the discourse.

Practice Exercises

☞   *Critical Question:* **What words or phrases are ambiguous?**

In the following passages, identify examples of ambiguity. Try to explain why the examples harm the reasoning.

Passage 1

We should treat drug taking in the same way we treat speech and religion, as a fundamental right. No one has to ingest any drug he does not want, just as no one has to read a particular book. Insofar as the state assumes control over such matters, it can only be in order to subjugate its citizens—by protecting them from temptations as befits children, and by preventing them from exercising self-determination over their lives as befits slaves.

Passage 2

Note: This passage is adapted from an opinion delivered by Chief Justice Warren Burger in a Supreme Court response concerning the constitutionality of a Georgia obscenity statute.

We categorically disapprove the theory, apparently adopted by the trial judge, that obscene, pornographic films acquire constitutional immunity from state regulation simply because they are exhibited for consenting adults only. This holding was properly rejected by the Georgia Supreme Court. . . . In particular, we hold that there are legitimate state interests at stake in stemming the tide of commercialized obscenity, even assuming it is feasible to enforce effective safeguards against exposure to juveniles and passersby. Rights and interests other than those of the advocates are involved. These include the interest of the public in the quality of life and the total community environment, the tone of commerce in the great city centers, and possibly, the public safety itself . . .

As Chief Justice Warren stated, there is a "right of the Nation and of the States to maintain a decent society. . . ," *Jacobellis v. Ohio,* 378 U.S. 184, 199 (1964) (dissenting opinion.) . . .

The sum of experience, including that of the past two decades, affords an ample basis for legislatures to conclude that a sensitive, key relationship of human existence, central to family life, community welfare and the development of human personality, can be debased and distorted by crass commercial exploitation of sex.

Passage 3

America has fallen behind in the utilization of nuclear energy plants. There are no new orders for nuclear power plants, yet other countries are building many such plants. America taught the world how to harness the atom. We simply cannot allow the rest of the world to walk away from us as leaders in this technology.

Nuclear power is safe, efficient, and necessary for our nation's future energy security. In the course of 800 reactor years, not a single member of the public has been injured or killed; and for more than 2,900 reactor years, American naval personnel have lived and worked alongside nuclear reactors traveling 60 million miles without a nuclear accident. No other technology can make similar claims; yet, the critics of nuclear energy persist in calling it unsafe. By any reasonable calculation nuclear power is going to be an essential generating source for American electricity in the next 30 years, and we must be ready to provide it.

Sample Responses

Passage 1

ISSUE: *Should the state regulate drug use?*

CONCLUSION: *Drug use should not be regulated by the state.*

REASONS: 1. *Just as freedom of speech and religion are fundamental rights, drug use should be a basic liberty.*
              2. *Because drug use is voluntary, the state has no right to intervene.*

What are the key phrases in this reasoning? They are: "drug taking," "fundamental right," and "subjugate citizens." You would first want to determine the meaning of each of these phrases. Is it clear what is meant by drug taking? No. The limited context provided fails to reveal an adequate definition. If drug taking refers to the ingestion of drugs that are not considered highly addictive, such as marijuana, wouldn't you be more likely to accept the reasoning than if the author included heroin within his definition of drugs? Can you tell from the argument whether the author is referring to all drugs or only to a subset of currently regulated drugs? To be able to agree or to disagree with the author requires in this instance a more careful definition of what is meant by *drugs.* Do any other words or phrases need further clarification before you can decide whether to agree with the author?

Passage 2

ISSUE: *Does the state have the right to regulate obscene materials?*

CONCLUSION: *Yes.*

REASONS: 1. *The nation and the states have a right to maintain a decent society.*
            2. *Experience proves that crass commercial exploitation of sex debases and distorts sexual relationships.*

The issue and conclusion jointly inform us that we are going to need to know what the author means by obscene materials before we can decide whether we want to agree with his arguments. Because the context we are given fails to clearly specify the meaning of *obscene,* we find it difficult to agree or disagree with the conclusion. Obscenity can have so many plausible meanings. For example, we might react differently to a definition emphasizing nudity than to a definition emphasizing perversity in sexual behavior. Thus obscenity is an important ambiguity in the context of this essay.

Several key phrases within the reasoning structure need clarification before we can evaluate the reasoning. Certainly, "maintaining a decent society" can have multiple meanings, and the author's reference to quality of life and total community environment, tone of commerce, and public safety is not as helpful as we would like. Given this language we would have a difficult time determining whether showing pornographic films "debases society." In fact, some might argue that restricting the right to show such films "debases society," because it restricts a "freedom."

We have a similar problem regarding the second reason. What is the meaning of debasing and distorting a sensitive key relationship? We think there are multiple plausible meanings, some that might be consistent with the impact of pornography and some that might not be.

Passage 3

ISSUE: *Should America increase its reliance on nuclear power?*

CONCLUSION: *America needs to build more nuclear power plants.*

REASONS: 1. *Nuclear power is safe, efficient, and necessary for our nation's future energy security.*
            2. *Nuclear power is going to be an essential generating source for American electricity in the next 30 years.*

Before we could adequately evaluate the first reason, we would like a clarification of "efficient" and "necessary"; and in the second reason, we would need to know more about the meaning of "essential generating source." Just how bad off are we likely to be in the next 30 years if we fail to build nuclear reactor plants? What makes a generating source "essential"?

Passage 4 (Self-Examination)

Universities should do more to prevent sexual harassment in the classroom. All across the campus, students are harassed by professors, and almost nothing ever happens to stop it.

Why does it happen? Professors have power over students, and many use that power to take advantage of their students. How convenient for the strong to misuse the weak in this fashion!

Even if the act of the harassment were not bad enough, the effects often decrease productivity and enthusiasm among victims. Then the very institution that failed to put a stop to the harassment turns around and judges students on their diminished productivity, the direct result of the harassment. How horribly unfair it is!

Think about this problem. If more female than male students are harassed in a sexual fashion, then more women students than male students will have the added burden of mastering their classes PLUS having to compensate for the psychological harm associated with the sexual harassment. On campuses on which there is the persistent threat of sexual harassment, it is truly remarkable that female students perform so well. Think what these same students could do without this problem of sexual harassment hanging over them.

5

What Are the Value Conflicts and Assumptions?

If potential murderers see convicted murderers receiving the death penalty, they will be deterred. If the potential murderer abducts your child and knows he will receive the death penalty if he kills her, won't he be more likely to leave her alone?

Let me change your example slightly. What if your son were walking to work one day and was falsely accused of murder? He is later convicted of murder and is executed. Has justice been served?

When someone is trying to convince you of her point of view, she may be shrewd. She will present reasons that are consistent with her position. That is why, at first glance, most arguments "make sense." The visible structure looks good. But the reasons that are *stated* are not the only ideas that the person is using to prove or support her opinion. Hidden or unstated thoughts may be at least as significant in understanding her argument. Let's examine the importance of these unstated ideas by considering the following brief argument.

> The government should prohibit the manufacture and sale of cigarettes. More and more evidence has demonstrated that smoking has harmful effects on the health of both the smoker and those exposed to smoking.

The reason—at first glance—supports the conclusion. If the government wants to prohibit a product, it makes sense that it should provide evidence that the product is bad. But it is also possible that the reason given can be true and yet *not necessarily* support the conclusion. What if you believe that it is the individual's responsibility—not the collective responsibility of government—to take care of his own welfare. If so, from your perspective, the reason no longer supports the conclusion. This reasoning is convincing to you only if you agree with certain unstated ideas that the writer has taken for granted. In this case, an idea taken for granted is that collective responsibility is more desirable than individual responsibility when an individual's welfare is threatened.

In all arguments, there will be certain ideas taken for granted by the writer. Typically, these ideas will not be stated. You will have to find them by reading between the lines. These ideas are important invisible links in the reasoning structure, the glue that holds the entire argument together. Until you supply these links, you cannot truly understand the argument.

Your task is similar in many ways to having to reproduce a magic trick without having seen how the magician did the trick. You see the handkerchief go into the hat and the rabbit come out, but you are not aware of the magician's hidden maneuvers. To understand the trick, you must discover these maneuvers. Likewise, in arguments, you must discover the hidden maneuvers, which, in actuality, are unstated ideas. We shall refer to these unstated ideas as *assumptions.* To fully understand an argument, you must identify the assumptions.

Assumptions are:

1. hidden or unstated (in most cases),
2. taken for granted,
3. influential in determining the conclusion,
4. necessary, if the reasoning is to make sense, and
5. potentially deceptive.

This chapter and the next one will show you how to discover assumptions. We will focus on one kind of assumption in this chapter—value assumptions.

☞ *Critical Question:* **What are the value conflicts and assumptions?**

General Guide for Identifying Assumptions

When you seek assumptions, where and how should you look? Numerous assumptions exist in any book, discussion, or article, but you need to be concerned about relatively few. As you remember, the visible structure of an argument is contained in reasons and conclusions. Thus, you are interested only in assumptions that affect the quality of this structure. You can restrict your search for assumptions, therefore, to the structure you have already learned how to identify. **Look for assumptions in the movement from reasons to conclusions!**

Attention: An assumption is an unstated belief that supports the explicit reasoning.

Value Conflicts and Assumptions

Why is it that some very reasonable people charge that abortion is murder, while other equally reasonable observers see abortion as humane? Have you ever wondered why every president, regardless of his political beliefs, eventually gets involved in a dispute with the press over publication of government information that he would prefer not to share? How can some highly intelligent observers attack the publication of sexually explicit magazines and others defend their publication as the ultimate test of our Bill of Rights?

One extremely important reason for these different conclusions is the existence of *value conflicts,* or the differing values that stem from different frames of reference. For ethical or prescriptive arguments, an individual's values influence the reasons he provides and, consequently, his conclusion. In fact, the reasons will logically support the conclusion only if the *value assumption* is added to the reasoning. The extract below illustrates the necessity that a value assumption be part of a prescriptive argument.

> We should not legalize recreational drugs. Illegal drugs cause too much street violence and other crimes.

Reason		*Value Assumption*
Illegal drugs cause violence and other crimes	+	Public safety is more important than freedom of choice

Conclusion
Therefore: Recreational drugs should not be legalized.

Value assumptions are, therefore, very important assumptions for such arguments. The person trying to communicate with you may or may not be aware of these assumptions. You should make it a habit to find out whether the value assumptions on which reasons are based are consistent with your own value assumptions before accepting or rejecting a conclusion.

Some of the most fundamental assumptions are those relating to value priorities. The rest of this chapter is devoted to increasing your awareness of the role played by value conflicts and value priorities in determining a person's opinions or conclusions. This awareness will help you to locate and evaluate this important type of assumption.

Discovering Values

Before you can discover the importance of values in shaping conclusions, you must have some understanding of what a value is. *Values,* as we will use the term,

---

Attention: Values are ideas that people see as worthwhile. They provide standards of conduct by which we measure the quality of human behavior.

are ideas that someone thinks are worthwhile. You will find that it is the importance one assigns to abstract *ideas* that has the major influence on one's choices and behavior. Usually objects, experiences, and actions are desired because of some idea we value. For example, we may choose to do things that provide us with contacts with important people. We probably value "important people" *because* we value "status." When we use the word *value* in this chapter, we will be referring to an idea representing what someone thinks is important and will strive to achieve.

To better familiarize yourself with values, write down some of your own values. Try to avoid writing down the names of people, tangible objects, or actions. Pizza and playing tennis may be important to you, but it is the importance you assign to ideas that most influences your choices and behavior concerning controversial public issues. Your willingness to argue for or against capital punishment, for instance, is strongly related to the importance you assign to the sanctity of human life—an abstract idea. The sanctity of human life is a value that affects our opinions about war, abortion, drug usage, and mercy killing. As you create your list of values, focus on those that are so significant that they affect your opinions and behavior in many ways.

Did you have problems making your list? We can suggest two further aids that may help. First, another definition! Values are *standards of conduct* that we endorse and expect people to meet. When we expect our political representatives to "tell the truth," we are indicating to them and to ourselves that honesty is one of our most cherished values. Ask yourself what you expect your friends to be like. What standards of conduct would you want your children to develop? Answers to these questions should help you enlarge your understanding of values.

When you are thinking about standards of conduct as a means of discovering values, recognize that certain conduct has an especially significant effect of your life. Certain values have a larger personal and social impact than others. Politeness, for instance, is a standard of conduct and a value, but it does not have the major impact on our lives that a value such as competition has. The point here is that certain values have greater consequences than others. Thus, you will usually want to focus on the values that most affect our behavior.

Now let us give you an aid for identifying values—a list of some commonly held values. Every value on our list may be an attractive candidate for your list. Thus, after you look at our list, pause for a moment and choose those values that are most important to you. They will be those values that most often play a role in shaping your opinions and behavior.

From Values to Value Assumptions

To identify value assumptions, we must go beyond a simple listing of values. Many of your values are shared by others. Wouldn't almost anyone claim that flexibility, cooperation, and honesty are desirable?

Common Values

adventure	equality of condition	novelty
ambition	equality of opportunity	order
autonomy	excellence	patriotism
collective responsibility	flexibility	peace
comfort	freedom of speech	rationality
competition	generosity	security
cooperation	harmony	spontaneity
courage	honesty	tolerance
creativity	justice	tradition
		wisdom

Look again at the definition, and you will immediately see that, *by definition,* most values will be on everyone's list. After all, these are ideas that are a reflection of our collective dreams as a species. Because many values are shared, values by themselves are not a powerful guide to understanding. What leads you to answer a prescriptive question differently from someone else is the relative intensity with which each of you holds specific values.

Difference in intensity of allegiance to particular values can easily be seen by thinking about responses to controversies when pairs of values collide or conflict. While it is not very enlightening to discover that most people value both competition and cooperation, we do gain a more complete understanding of prescriptive choices as we discover who *prefers* competition to cooperation when the two values conflict.

A writer's preferences for particular values are often unstated, but they will have a major impact on her conclusion and on how she chooses to defend it. These unstated assertions about value priorities function as *value assumptions.* Some refer to these assumptions as *value judgments.* Recognition of relative support for conflicting values or sets of values provides you with both an improved understanding of what you are reading and a basis for eventual evaluation of prescriptive arguments.

When a writer takes a stand on controversial prescriptive issues, he is usually depreciating one commonly shared value while upholding another. For example, when someone advocates the required licensing of prospective parents, collective responsibility is being treated as more important than individual responsibility. So when you look for value assumptions, look for an indication of value preferences. Ask yourself what values are being upheld by this position and what values are being depreciated.

Attention: A value assumption is an implicit preference for one value over another in a particular context.

Caution: When we evaluate arguments, we are not helped tremendously by simply discovering the values implicit in the argument. No standard of rationality is violated just because an argument depends on specific values. But once we identify the value preferences or assumptions on which an argument is leaning, we certainly do have an opportunity to make a judgment about the reasoning. The failure of a communicator to justify those value assumptions when they differ from your own is definitely a basis for your hesitancy to accept an argument. Notice that it would have been unfair to simply say that any argument based on different value assumptions than those you tend to hold is thereby unacceptable. You want to give others a chance to be heard; maybe you can learn from them. But you have every right to expect a person to persuade you that those different assumptions are appropriate in this instance. When no response is forthcoming, you can reasonably reject the argument, at least for now.

DYNAMITE

When you have found a person's value preference in a particular argument, you should not expect that same person to necessarily have the same value priority when discussing a different controversy. A person does not have the same value priorities without regard to the issue being discussed. The reason is that the context and factual issues associated with a controversy also greatly influence how far we're willing to go with a particular value preference. We hold our value preferences *only up to a point*. Thus, for example, those who prefer freedom of choice over the welfare of the community in most situations (such as wearing clothing that includes a picture of the flag) may shift that value preference when they see the possibility of too much damage to the welfare of the community (such as in the case of the right of a person to give a racist speech.)

Typical Value Conflicts

If you are aware of typical conflicts, you can more quickly recognize the assumptions being made by a writer when she reaches a particular conclusion. We have listed some of the more common value conflicts that occur in ethical issues and have provided you with examples of controversies in which these value conflicts are likely to be evident. We anticipate that you can use this list as a starting point when you are trying to identify important value assumptions.

As you identify value conflicts, you will often find that there are several value conflicts that seem important in shaping conclusions with respect to particular controversies. When evaluating a controversy, try to find several value conflicts, as a check on yourself. Some controversies will have one primary value conflict; others may have several.

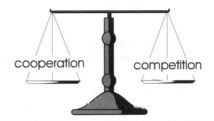

Typical Value Conflicts and Sample Controversies

1. loyalty—honesty	1. Should you tell your parents about your sister's drug habit?
2. competition—cooperation	2. Do you support the grading system?
3. freedom of press—national security	3. Is it wise to hold weekly presidential press conferences?
4. equality—individualism	4. Are racial quotas for employment fair?
5. order—freedom of speech	5. Should we imprison those with radical ideas?
6. security—excitement	6. Should you choose a dangerous profession?
7. generosity—material success	7. Is it desirable to give financial help to a beggar?
8. rationality—spontaneity	8. Should you check the odds before placing a bet?
9. tradition—novelty	9. Should divorces be easily available?

Take another look at number 7 in the preceding list. It is quite possible that value conflicts besides that between generosity and material success affect your decision about whether to give financial help to a beggar. For instance, all the following value conflicts may affect a person's willingness to help a beggar:

1. individual responsibility—collective responsibility
2. competition—cooperation
3. efficiency—social stability

By identifying as many of the relevant value assumptions as possible, you have a better chance of not missing any of the important dimensions of the argument. However, you may have no way of knowing which value assumptions are actually responsible for the author's conclusion.

The Communicator's Background As a Clue to Value Assumptions

It has already been suggested that a good starting point in finding value assumptions is to check the background of the author. Find out as much as you can about the value preferences usually held by a person like the writer. Is he a corporate executive, a union leader, a Republican Party official, a doctor, or an apartment tenant? What interests does such a person naturally wish to protect? There's certainly nothing inherently wrong with pursuing self-interest, but such pursuits often limit the value assumptions a particular writer will tolerate. For example, it's highly unlikely that the president of a major automobile firm would place a high value on efficiency when a preference for efficiency rather than stability would lead to his losing his job. Consequently, you as a critical reader or listener can often quickly discover value preferences by thinking about the probable assumptions made by a person like the writer.

One caution is important. It isn't necessarily true that, because a writer is a member of a group, she shares the particular value assumptions of the group. It would be a mistake to presume that every individual who belongs to a given group thinks identically. We all know that people in business, farmers, and firefighters sometimes disagree among themselves when discussing particular controversies. Investigating the writer's background as a clue to her value assumptions is only a clue, and, like other clues, it can be misleading unless it is used with care.

Consequences As Clues to Value Assumptions

In prescriptive arguments, each position with respect to an issue leads to different consequences or outcomes. Each of the potential consequences will have a certain likelihood of occurring, and each will also have some level of desirability or undesirability. How desirable a consequence is will depend on a writer's or reader's personal value preferences. The desirability of the conclusions in such cases will be dictated by the probability of the potential consequences and the importance attached to them. Thus, an important means of determining an individual's value assumptions is to examine the reasons given in support of a conclusion and then to determine what value preferences would lead to these reasons being judged as more desirable than reasons that might have been offered on the other side of the issue. Let's take a look at a concrete example.

Nuclear power plants should not be built because they will pollute our environment.

The reason provided here is a rather specific potential consequence of building nuclear plants. This writer clearly sees environmental pollution as very undesirable. Why does this consequence carry so much weight in this person's thinking? What more general value does preventing pollution help achieve? Probably conservation, or perhaps naturalness. Someone else might stress a different consequence in this argument, such as the effect on the supply of electricity to consumers. Why? Probably because he values efficiency very highly. Thus, this reason supports the conclusion *if* a value assumption is made that conservation is more important than efficiency.

Note that the *magnitude* of a consequence may have a major impact on value preferences. One may value conservation over efficiency only when efficiency may cause "significant" damage to the environment. And, one may value free enterprise over economic security only as long as unemployment stays below a given level.

It is possible for people to have different conclusions, while having identical value assumptions, because they disagree about the likelihood or magnitude of consequences.

One important means of determining value assumptions, then, is to ask the question, "Why do the particular consequences or outcomes presented as reasons seem so desirable to the writer or speaker?"

Remember: When you identify *value assumptions,* you should always try to state *value preferences.* With controversial topics, stating value assumptions in this way will be a continual reminder both of what the writer is *giving up* and of what she is gaining.

More Hints for Finding Value Assumptions

Many social controversies share important characteristics; they are thus *analogous* to one another. The value preferences implicit in a certain controversy can sometimes be discovered by searching for analogous elements in other social controversies. Do any common characteristics have their origin in a similar value conflict?

Let's ask, for instance, how a particular controversy is similar to other controversies, and see whether the answer gives us a clue to an important value assumption.

Should the government require car manufacturers to include air bags in automobiles?

What are the important characteristics of this controversy? The controversy, more generally, asks whether collective groups, such as the government, should intervene in people's lives to help them protect themselves. Such an intervention is analogous to banning cigarette advertising, requiring motorcycle riders to wear helmets, and banning boxing. Once you have recognized the similarity of these issues, you should be able to see how certain values will dictate individuals' positions on them. Someone who believes that the government should require air bags in cars is also likely to believe that the government should ban cigarette advertising. Why? Because he values collective responsibility and public safety more than individual responsibility.

Should it be legal for newspaper and television reporters to refuse to reveal their confidential sources?

How did you do? We thought of the question of whether psychiatrists should be allowed to refuse to testify about their patients in murder trials. Whatever different examples you thought of, our guess is that your thinking made you aware of some important values, such as privacy, the public's right to know, or public safety. Awareness of value conflicts is a necessary step toward determining value assumptions.

Another useful technique for generating value conflicts is to *reverse role-play*. Ask the question, "What do those people who would take a different position from the writer's care about?" When someone argues that we should not use monkeys in experimental research, you should ask yourself, "If I wanted to defend the use of monkeys, what would I be concerned about?" Remember, when someone takes a position on a controversial topic, she will be revealing a *value preference*. Your knowledge of that preference will help you to decide whether to agree with her conclusion.

Finally, you can always check to see whether the disagreement results from a value conflict concerning the *rights of an individual* to behave in a particular fashion and the *welfare of the group* affected by the behavior in question. Many arguments rest implicitly on a stance with respect to this enduring value conflict. Like other common value conflicts, we can all recall numerous instances when our thinking requires us to weigh these two important values and their effects.

For example, when we wonder about the merit of mandatory drug-testing in the workplace, we often begin to construct our arguments in terms of thinking about the privacy rights of the individual workers *and* the threats to the community that might result from a worker's drug-related judgment error. Then, we try to balance those values: Does the individual's right to privacy deserve greater protection than the welfare of the community in this instance? What other issues involve this value conflict? What about the request of skinheads to parade through ethnic neighborhoods?

Finding Value Assumptions on Your Own

Let's work on an example together to help you become more comfortable with finding value assumptions.

Congress is attempting to pass legislation that will reduce the level of commercial exploitation currently present in children's television. The proposal calls for limitations on the number and type of commercials permitted during children's programming. This proposal has met with great opposition from those who insist that parents, not legislators, should monitor TV. They maintain that parents alone must take responsibility for their children's TV viewing.

Supporters of the proposal, however, point out that children's shows have turned into half-hour commercials. They insist that government regulation is necessary to protect children from the blatant exploitation of commercialism. They demand that children's programming respect the special needs and relative immaturity of the young, rather than manipulate them for profit.

The structure of the two positions is outlined here for you:

CONCLUSION: *The government should not regulate children's television programming.*

REASON: *Parents should be the source of any such regulation.*

CONCLUSION: *The government should regulate children's programming.*

REASON: *Children are especially vulnerable to exploitation by those wishing to profit from television programming.*

Notice that the opposition reasons that regulation is undesirable because it infringes on the individual parent's responsibility to monitor the TV. They believe that it is up to the individual to decide what is and is not desirable. Thus, government regulation impinges on one's individual responsibility for monitoring what happens in their own homes.

VALUE ASSUMPTION: *In this context, individual responsibility is more important than collective responsibility.*

On the other hand, supporters of the proposal insist that help from an instrument of the community, such as the government, is necessary for the greater good of the nation's children. They believe that a reduction in the exploitation of children is worth a minor cutback in individual responsibility. They think that the collective action of the government can more effectively reduce exploitation than the efforts of individuals.

VALUE ASSUMPTION: *In this situation, collective responsibility is more important than personal responsibility.*

Therefore, the major value conflict is collective responsibility versus individual responsibility. A supporter of the proposal makes the value assumption that laws that will protect children are more important than unchecked individual responsibility. Her stance on this issue does not mean that she does not value individual responsibility; both values are probably very important to her. In this case, however, collective responsibility has taken priority. Similarly, opponents of the proposal do not advocate the exploitation of children. In this case, they believe that the preservation of individual responsibility takes precedence over collective action.

Remember that complete reasoning with respect to prescriptive issues requires reasons *and* value assumptions.

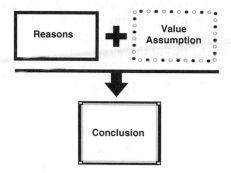

Let's complete one more example together.

Students should obey a dress code that includes uniforms, shoe restrictions, and hair length. In such an educational setting, teachers can teach and students can learn. Valuable time and energy will not be wasted on the discipline problems that arise in the absence of a rigid dress code.

Let's first outline the structure of the argument.

CONCLUSION: *Students should obey a rigid dress code.*

REASON: *Discipline problems would be reduced as a result of obedience to such a code.*

What value assumption do you think would result in someone's support for a rigid dress code for the schools? Look back at the table on page 57. Would any of the sample value conflicts affect one's reaction to school dress codes and the use of the above reasoning? Try to explain how a preference for educational excellence over individual self-expression might affect your reaction to this controversy.

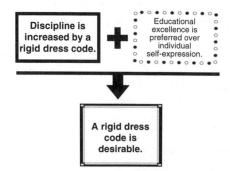

Identifying value assumptions is not only necessary to understand why someone makes a particular claim, but it will also help you relate to the various conclusions arrived at by the same individual. As we try to understand one another, it is sometimes helpful to recognize patterns in our behavior. One key to patterns of human behavior is an appreciation of value conflicts. Although you cannot be sure, it is a good first guess to predict that those who prefer to see campus police with weapons will also favor a hard-line approach to negotiations with Iraq, spanking as a form of discipline, and tougher jail sentences for juvenile delinquents.

Caution: Don't get so involved with identifying value assumptions that you forget why you are searching for them. As with any assumption, there is absolutely nothing improper about basing reasons on assumptions. In fact, you must do so yourself. Assumptions are an essential element of reasoning. You are trying to find the value assumptions to see whether you are comfortable with that assumption yourself. As a reader, all you can do is voice skepticism about the argument because the author is not present to provide the missing defense.

DYNAMITE

Summary

Assumptions are unstated ideas, taken for granted in the reasoning. Value assumptions are one type of unstated idea, consisting of a preference for one value over another in a particular context. The author's background, reaction to projected consequences of acting on a particular value assumption, analogous controversies, and reverse role-playing all provide possible clues for finding a person's value assumptions in a particular controversy.

Practice Exercises

☞ *Critical Question:* ***What are the value conflicts and assumptions?***

Identify the value conflicts that could lead to agreement or disagreement with the following points of view, then identify the value priorities assumed by the writer.

Passage 1

Some members of our society receive outrageous sums of money each year. Athletes, entertainers, and executives receive incomes that most of us can hardly imagine. At the same time, in the same country, other people are unable to heat their homes, afford nutritious meals, or finance automobiles. No one should be allowed to make a salary that is 100 times larger than that of the average person.

Passage 2

I would not like to see women in combat. If a war breaks out, all of us want only the most qualified people to be fighting for our country. I fear that women would not be able to handle the emotional strains involved in battle. Their strength as humans is in caring and nurturing. Let's let them do what they can do best.

And, just to show that I have no gender bias against women, I want to point out that men are too weak to fight when women are present. They would be distracted by the desire to protect their female comrades. Men are weak in this regard. In conclusion, the needs of women, men, and our country in general speak against permitting women to go into combat.

Passage 3

For most people, college is a waste of time and money. One does not need schools to learn. If you go to college to make it possible to earn more money, you have been had. More than half of those who earn more than $35,000 never received a college diploma. What you do learn in college is rarely useful on the job. Most of you would be better off saving part of the money you earn while your naïve friends are in college.

Sample Responses

Passage 1

CONCLUSION: *No one should make more than 100 times the salary of the average worker.*

REASON: *The gap between rich and poor is preventing some Americans from having basic necessities.*

One value conflict that would cause readers to disagree is that between equal opportunity and equality of condition. The argument depends on the importance of everyone's having the basic necessities. The existence of huge incomes limits the amount of money left over for others to buy those necessities. Hence those who value equality of condition more than equality of opportunity may well argue that regardless of the similar opportunities available to all workers, each of us should be guaranteed a basic level of goods and services. The value assumption links the reason to the conclusion.

Passage 2

CONCLUSION: *Women should not be permitted in combat situations.*

REASONS: 1. *They lack the necessary emotional toughness.*
2. *Their comparative strength lies elsewhere, in nurturing and caring.*
3. *Men are so weak that they would be unable to fight well if women were in combat, for they would feel the need to protect female soldiers.*

One value conflict that relates to this argument is between tradition and equality of opportunity. Women have not traditionally been in combat situations in our country. Yet, we know that some women seek this opportunity. Men have it; the women applicants quite understandably say, "What about us?" The author makes the standard traditional arguments against using women in combat: They aren't up to it; they do a greater service at home; and they provide a dangerous distraction to our male troops on the battlefield. A value preference for tradition over equality of opportunity links the reasons to the conclusion.

As with most prescriptive controversies, more than one value conflict is involved in this dilemma. For example, this controversy also requires us to think about the rights of the individual versus the welfare of the community, as well as the tension between ambition and comfort.

Passage 3

CONCLUSION: *Most young people should not attend college.*

REASONS: 1. *Many of those who make a lot of money never attend college.*
2. *College does not generally teach job-related skills.*

A value assumption is that materialistic achievement is more important than wisdom. Notice that the consequences stressed by the author is the impact of college on future income. She addresses none of the other purposes one might have for attending college. If one valued wisdom more than monetary accumulation, one might well reject the reasoning suggested in this passage.

Passage 4 (Self-Examination)

America's youth are being cheated out of their educational future by narrow-minded budget cuts. Legislatures have apparently forgotten that learning requires a network of support and that those who facilitate the learning process require resources to do their jobs effectively. Unless teachers feel that their work is appreciated, they may find it hard to get up each day, excited about the challenge of encouraging as much learning as they know how.

Direct federal support for students is one more area where the cutbacks are harmful. When students cannot afford higher education, they certainly lose, but so do we all. The creativity and talents that would have been developed through higher education are lost to all of us. Just because a student is not born into a rich family, should they be unable to attend college? Where is our sense of justice and opportunity?

6

What Are the Descriptive Assumptions?

You should now be able to identify value assumptions—very important hidden links in prescriptive arguments. When you find value assumptions, you know pretty well what a writer or speaker wants the world to be like—what ideals he thinks are most important to strive for. But you do not know what he takes for granted about what the world was, is, or will be like. His visible reasoning depends on these ideas, as well as upon his values. Such unstated ideas are *descriptive assumptions,* and they are essential hidden links in an argument.

A brief argument concerning Professor Starr depends on such hidden assumptions. Can you find them?

You will learn a lot from Professor Starr. His students all rave about his lectures.

This chapter focuses on the identification of descriptive assumptions.

☞   *Critical Question:* **What are the descriptive assumptions?**

Descriptive assumptions are beliefs about the way the world *is;* prescriptive or value assumptions, you remember, are beliefs about how the world *should be.*

Illustrating Descriptive Assumptions

Let's examine our argument about Professor Starr more closely to illustrate more clearly what we mean by a descriptive assumption.

The reasoning structure is:

CONCLUSION: *You will learn a lot from Professor Starr.*

REASON: *His students all rave about his lectures.*

The reasoning thus far is incomplete. We know that, *by itself,* a reason cannot support a conclusion; the reason must be connected to the conclusion by certain other (frequently unstated) ideas. These ideas are ones, which if true, justify treating the reason as support for the conclusion. Thus, whether a reason supports, or is relevant to, a conclusion depends on whether we can locate unstated ideas that logically connect the reason to the conclusion. When such unstated ideas are descriptive, we choose to call them *descriptive connecting assumptions.* Let us present two such assumptions for the above argument.

ASSUMPTION 1: *Student comments are a good indicator of lecture quality.*

First, note that *if* the reason is true and *if* this assumption is true, then the reason provides some support for the conclusion. If students, however, rave about lectures because of their entertainment value rather than because of their contribution to wisdom, then the reason given is not supportive of the conclusion. Next, note that this assumption is a statement about the way things *are,* not about the way things *should be.* Thus, it is a *descriptive assumption.*

ASSUMPTION 2: *To learn a lot means to absorb material from a lecture.*

(Sponge model thinking, right?) If "learn a lot" is defined as developing thinking skills, then the amount of raving about lectures may be irrelevant. Thus, this conclusion is supported by the reason only if a certain definition of learning is assumed.

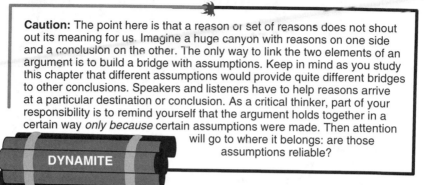

Caution: The point here is that a reason or set of reasons does not shout out its meaning for us. Imagine a huge canyon with reasons on one side and a conclusion on the other. The only way to link the two elements of an argument is to build a bridge with assumptions. Keep in mind as you study this chapter that different assumptions would provide quite different bridges to other conclusions. Speakers and listeners have to help reasons arrive at a particular destination or conclusion. As a critical thinker, part of your responsibility is to remind yourself that the argument holds together in a certain way *only because* certain assumptions were made. Then attention will go to where it belongs: are those assumptions reliable?

We can call this kind of descriptive assumption a *definitional assumption* because we have taken for granted one meaning of a term that could have more than one meaning. Thus, one important kind of descriptive assumption to look for is a definitional assumption—the taking for granted of one meaning for a term that has multiple possible meanings. Let's see what this looks like in argument form:

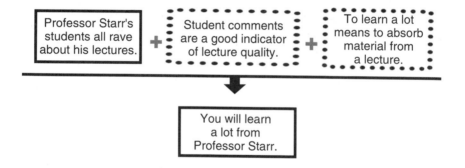

Once you have identified the connecting assumptions, you have answered the question, "On what basis can that conclusion be drawn from that reason?" The next natural step is to ask, "Is there any basis for accepting the assumptions?" If not, then, for you, the reason fails to provide support for the conclusion. If so, then the reason provides logical support for the conclusion. Many label such reasoning *valid reasoning*. Thus, you can say reasoning is valid when you have identified connecting assumptions and you have good reason to believe those assumptions.

Attention: A descriptive assumption is an unstated belief about how the world was, is, or will become.

Note that there are further hidden assumptions in the above argument. For example, you should not be convinced by this reasoning unless you believe that the qualities others look for in lectures are the same qualities you look for. Should you eat at a restaurant because many of your friends rave about it? Wouldn't you want to know *why* they rave about it? *Remember:* Reasoning will usually contain multiple assumptions.

Note also that when you identify assumptions, you identify ideas the communicator *needs* to take for granted for the reason to be supportive of the conclusion. Because writers and speakers frequently are not aware of their own assumptions, their conscious beliefs may be quite different from the ideas you identify as implicit assumptions.

Clues for Locating Assumptions

Your job in finding assumptions is to reconstruct the reasoning by filling in the missing gaps. That is, you want to provide ideas that help the communicator's reasoning "make sense." Once you have a picture of the entire argument, both the visible and the invisible parts, you will be in a much better position to determine its strengths and weaknesses.

How does one go about finding these important missing links? It requires hard work, imagination, and creativity. Finding important assumptions is a difficult task.

You have been introduced to two types of assumptions—value assumptions and descriptive assumptions. In the previous chapter, we gave you several hints for finding value assumptions. Here are some clues that will make your search for descriptive assumptions successful.

Keep thinking about the gap between the conclusion and reasons.   Why are you looking for assumptions in the first place? You are looking because you want to be able to judge how well the reasons support the conclusions. Thus, look for what the writer or speaker would have had to take for granted to link the reasons and conclusion. Keep asking, *"How do you get from the reason to the conclusion?"* Ask, *"If the reason is true, what else must be true for the conclusion to follow?"* And, to help answer that question, you will find it very helpful to ask, *"Supposing the reason(s) were true, is there any way in which the conclusion nevertheless could be false?"*

Searching for the gap will be helpful for finding both value and descriptive assumptions.

Look for ideas that support reasons.   Sometimes a reason is presented with no explicit support; yet the plausibility of the reason depends on the acceptability of ideas taken for granted. These ideas are descriptive assumptions. The following brief argument illustrates such a case:

CONCLUSION: *We need to increase the money spent on AIDS education.*

REASON: *If we do so, it will greatly reduce the number of cases of AIDS.*

What ideas must be taken for granted for this reason to be acceptable? We must assume:

(a) the money will be spent in an effective manner; in other words, the education will reach members of high-risk groups that are not already being reached, and

(b) such members will be willing and able to respond to the educational message.

Thus, both (a) and (b) are ideas that have to be taken for granted for the reasons to be acceptable, and thus supportive of the conclusion.

Identify with the writer or speaker.   Locating someone's assumptions is often made easier by imagining that you were asked to defend the conclusion. If you can, crawl into the skin of a person who would reach such a conclusion. Discover his background. Whether the person whose conclusion you are evaluating is a corporate executive, a communist, a labor leader, a boxing promoter, or a judge, try to play the role of such a person and plan in your mind what he would be thinking as he moves toward the conclusion. When an executive for a coal company argues that strip mining does not significantly harm the beauty of our natural environment, he has probably begun with a belief that strip mining is beneficial to our nation. Thus, he may assume a definition of beauty that would be consistent with his arguments, while other definitions of beauty would lead to a condemnation of strip mining.

Identify with the opposition.   If you are unable to locate assumptions by taking the role of the speaker or writer, try to reverse roles. Ask yourself why anyone might disagree with the conclusion. What type of reasoning would prompt someone to disagree with the conclusion you are evaluating? If you can play the role of a person who would not accept the conclusion, you can more readily see assumptions in the original structure.

Recognize the potential existence of other means of attaining the advantages referred to in the reasons.   Frequently, a conclusion is supported by reasons that indicate the various advantages of acting on the author's conclusion. When there are many ways to reach the same advantages, one important assumption linking the reasons to the conclusion is that the best way to attain the advantages is through the one advocated by the communicator.

Let's try this technique with one brief example. Many counselors would argue that a college freshman should be allowed to choose her own courses without any restrictions from parents or college personnel because it facilitates the growth of personal responsibility. But aren't there many ways to encourage the growth of personal responsibility? Might not some of these alternatives have less serious disadvantages than those that could result when a freshman makes erroneous judgments about which courses would be in her best long-term interest? For example, the development of personal responsibility is furthered by requiring a student to make a substantial financial contribution to the cost of her education. Thus, those who argue that it is desirable to permit college freshman to make their own course choices because such an opportunity encourages personal responsibility are assuming that there are not less risky alternatives for accomplishing a similar goal.

Learn more about issues.   The more familiar you are with all sides of a topic, the more easily you will be able to locate assumptions. Get as much information about the issues that you care about as you can.

Avoid stating incompletely established reasons as assumptions.   When you first attempt to locate assumptions you may find yourself locating a stated reason, thinking that the reason has not been adequately established, and asserting, "That's only an assumption. You don't know that to be the case." Or you might simply restate the reason as the assumption. You may have correctly identified a need on the part of the writer or speaker to better establish the truth of his reason. While this is an important insight on your part, you have not identified an assumption in the sense that we have been using it in these two chapters. You are simply labeling a reason "an assumption."

Here is an example of stating an incompletely established reason as an assumption.

> High salaries are ruining professional sports, and a major reason is that the high salaries are alienating fans.

Now, challenge the argument by identifying the following assumption: *The writer is assuming that high salaries really are alienating fans.*

Do you see that when you do this, all you are doing is stating that the author's reason is her assumption—when what you are probably really trying to stress is that the author's reason has not been sufficiently established by evidence.

Applying the Clues

Let's look at an argument about the impact of rock music and see whether we can identify descriptive and value assumptions.

> The immense attraction of rock music for college students is having a negative impact on their scholarship. Books no longer claim the enthusiasm that is now directed to the rock star of the week. How can we expect students to struggle with a lengthy passage from Plato when they have become accustomed to experiencing

the throbbing, pulsating, primitive excitement of rock music? Such music provides premature ecstasy—like a drug—an instant ecstasy that books and the classroom cannot provide them. Furthermore, with the prevalence of the portable cassette and CD players, students can be constantly plugged into music. With so much time devoted to music (the hour spent in line for concert tickets, the concerts themselves, not to mention listening time alone), studies must suffer.

Not only is rock music competing for our students' attention, but, increasingly, students are turning to rock for answers to both personal and universal problems. The socially conscious rock star is the new hero of the young. The solutions offered by such rock stars, however, are guilty of oversimplification. The weighty problems of the day cannot be adequately addressed in a five-minute lyric. Nevertheless, students are absorbing the words of millionaire musicians with far more reverence than they display toward their lessons or professors.

CONCLUSION: *Rock music is having a negative impact on college learning.*

REASONS: 1. *Books require much contemplative effort; they thus can't compete with the easy, instant gratification provided by rock music.*
2. *Attention directed to rock music diverts attention from studies.*
3. *Students are absorbing the oversimplified messages of the music rather than the complex ideas of their professors.*

First, note that the author provides no "proof" for her reasons. Thus, you might be tempted to state, "Those reasons are only assumptions; she does not know that." Wrong! They are not *assumptions! Remember:* identifying less-than-fully established reasons, though important, is *not* the same as identifying assumptions—ideas that are taken for granted as a basic part of the argument.

Now, let's see whether any descriptive assumptions can be found in the argument. Remember to keep thinking about the gap between the conclusion and the reasons as you look. First, ask yourself, "Is there any basis for believing that the reason(s) might not be true?" Then ask, "Supposing the reason(s) were true, is there any way in which the conclusion nevertheless could be false?" Try to play the role of a person who is strongly attracted to rock music.

Look at the first two reasons. Neither would be true if it were the case that excitement of the passions and excitement of the intellect can work in harmony rather than in disharmony. Perhaps listening to rock music reduces tension for students such that they are less distracted when they are engaged in intellectual effort. Thus, one descriptive assumption is that *listening to rock music does not provide a relaxation effect.* Also, for the second reason to be true, it would have to be the case *that the time used for rock music is time that would otherwise be devoted to scholarly effort* (descriptive assumption). Perhaps the time devoted to rock music is "surplus time" for students.

Let's now suppose that the first two reasons were true. Rock music still might not have a negative impact on learning if it is the case that students are so motivated to learn that they will make an effort to overcome any potential negative effects. Thus, an assumption connecting the first two reasons to the conclusion is that *students are not sufficiently motivated to learn to overcome the obstacles posed by rock music's attraction.* Another connecting assumption is that *those who listen often to rock music are the same students who would be interested in scholarly activity.*

Consider the third reason. It is true only if it is the case that students process the messages of rock music just as they might process book and classroom messages. Perhaps the messages are processed as "entertainment," in the way a roller-coaster ride is processed. Thus, an important assumption is that *students fail to discriminate between messages provided by rock music and those provided by the classroom.*

Note also that there is a prescriptive quality to this essay; thus, important value assumptions underlie the reasoning. What is the author concerned about preserving? Try reverse role-playing. What would someone who disagreed with this position care about? What are the advantages to young people of listening to rock music? Your answers to these questions should lead you to the essay's value preference. For example, can you see how a preference for the cultivation of the intellect over gratification of the senses links the reasons to the conclusion?

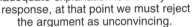

Caution: Finding descriptive assumptions is a difficult enough task that it is tempting to be satisfied with a job well done after identifying a few in an argument. But why were we looking for them in the first place? How does our finding them help us to evaluate arguments—our real task?

If we have some questions about the accuracy of the descriptive assumptions, we will want to voice these concerns and follow with a request for justification. Our approach should be to give the person making the argument an opportunity to explain to us why the assumption is one on which we can depend. If an inadequate explanation is the only response, at that point we must reject the argument as unconvincing.

DYNAMITE

Avoiding Analysis of Trivial Assumptions

Writers and speakers take for granted certain self-evident things about which we should not concern ourselves. You will want to devote your energy to evaluating important assumptions, so we want to warn you about some potential trivial assumptions.

You as a reader or listener can assume that the writer believes his reasons are true. You may want to attack the reasons as insufficient, but it is trivial to point out the writer's assumption that they are true.

Another type of trivial assumption concerns the reasoning structure. You may be tempted to state that the writer believes that the reason and conclusion are logically related. Right—but trivial. What is important is *how* they are logically related. It is also trivial to point out that an argument assumes that we can understand the logic, that we can understand the terminology, or that we have the appropriate background knowledge.

Avoid spending time on analyzing trivial assumptions. Your search for assumptions will be most rewarding when you locate hidden, debatable missing links.

Summary

Assumptions are ideas that, if true, enable us to claim that particular reasons provide support for a conclusion. Several clues aid in discovering descriptive assumptions:

1. Keep thinking about the gap between the conclusion and reasons.
2. Look for ideas that support reasons.
3. Identify with the opposition.
4. Recognize the potential existence of other means of attaining the advantages referred to in the reasons.
5. Learn more about the issues.

Practice Exercises

☞   *Critical Question:* **What are the descriptive assumptions?**

For each of the three passages, locate important assumptions made by the author. Remember first to determine the conclusion and the reasons.

Passage 1

Those who try to fight the use of animals in medical experiments often harm their own cause. Their tactics create more enemies than friends. Pouring blood on a researcher's car or breaking into laboratories to "liberate" animals is too extreme to attract respect for their cause. To be believable as a spokesperson for kindness and humanity, one must represent reason and humility. Argument, not physical coercion, will accomplish a deserved objective. A seminar is more productive in helping such animals than are all the shouting and violence used by animal rights activists.

Passage 2

Should it be legal for newspaper and television reporters to refuse to reveal their confidential sources? Indeed it should. The reporter-informant relationship is, after all, similar to those of priest and penitent, lawyer and client, physician and patient—all of which have a degree of privacy under the law. Moreover, if that relationship were not protected, the sources of information needed by the public would dry up.

Passage 3

Critical-thinking programs will not work. Critical-thinking skills should be taught like all other bodily skills, by coaching, not by combining lectures with textbooks that claim to teach people specific thinking skills. After all, we don't teach doctors and lawyers how to think critically by giving them a course in critical thinking. We require them to use critical-thinking skills in all courses that they are taught. We teach them by coaching, by providing lots of practice and corrective feedback.

Thinking is not a skill that can be taught in isolation from other mental acts and from the content of our disciplines. Instead of developing critical-thinking programs, we should be making sure that our students are coached in critical thinking in all their courses. If all our teachers would act as coaches and require our students to think about what is being taught instead of having them memorizing the facts, then we would not need critical-thinking courses.

Sample Responses

In presenting assumptions for the following arguments, we will list only *some* of the assumptions being made—those which we believe are among the most significant.

Passage 1

CONCLUSION: *Animal rights advocates have chosen a poor strategy.*

REASONS: 1. *The public reacts negatively to dramatic or illegal efforts to achieve an objective.*
2. *Because such advocates are claiming the moral high ground, they, too, must be above moral reproach.*
3. *Argument achieves objectives more effectively than does direct physical intervention.*

To be acceptable, the first reason requires the descriptive assumption that the public does not believe in civil disobedience as a legitimate stimulus for change. In this instance, the public may be so repulsed by the use of animals in medical experiments that they are not bothered by dramatic or even illegal behavior by animal rights advocates.

For the second reason to support the conclusion, the reasoning must assume that the immorality of those who seek to end the use of animals in medical experiments is perceived by the public. Alleged immoral tactics will not have a negative effect on the intended objective if the public isn't even aware of the tactics.

Passage 2

CONCLUSION: *It should be legal for newspaper and television reporters to refuse to reveal their confidential sources.*

REASONS: 1. *The reporter-informant relationship is special.*
2. *If the relationship is not protected, sources of information will dry up.*

The author compares the reporter-informant relationship to others. The first reason will be less acceptable if the reasons for privacy of lawyer and client or physician and patient are quite different from what they are for the reporter-informant relationship. For example, reporters, unlike these other professionals, regularly make their information public, creating a number of social consequences for individuals in society.

A major assumption necessary for the second reason to be acceptable is that most of the information reporters rely on for their stories comes from sources who would be so severely frightened by the threat of being revealed that they would refuse to provide information. It may be the case that many individuals would still come forth to provide information because they could tolerate the risk.

Passage 3

CONCLUSION: *Critical-thinking programs will not work.*

REASON: *Such skills can be better taught by coaching students within their respective disciplines.*
a. Lawyers and physicians are taught by coaching, not by critical-thinking courses.
b. Thinking cannot be taught apart from the content of a discipline.

Try reverse role-playing, taking the position of someone who teaches a critical-thinking course, perhaps using *Asking the Right Questions*.

For the reason to support the conclusion, it must be true that most critical-thinking courses do rely on lectures, not on coaching, or on practice of the skills.

Does the example support the reason? It does if the procedures used to train lawyers and physicians to think are successful. Perhaps these professionals could benefit greatly from a critical-thinking course that focuses on basic skills.

This entire argument rests on the assumption that it is not helpful to later coaching to have a good grounding in the basic skills. Coaching might be most successful in cases in which the learner has been explicitly taught the basic skills at an earlier time. There is also a "wishful thinking" assumption implied by the statement that lawyers and physicians are taught by coaching. Because students *need* coaching in all courses does not mean they will necessarily get such coaching.

Passage 4 (Self-Examination)

I'd like to try to get a point through the hard heads of those pushing to raise the legal drinking age. Their behavior is designed to make more young men and women law violators. When I was 18, I drank beer when it was against the law, and if I had to do it all over again, knowing myself at 18, I'd probably do it all over again. And, I don't think I was different from a lot of 18-year-olds.

If young people are old enough to go to Saudi Arabia, they are old enough to take a legal drink. If they are old enough to own property, drive cars, hold jobs, have children, raise them, and pay taxes, then they are old enough to take a drink.

Have we really given up on education? Have we given up on teachers and preachers and parents who are supposed to teach our young how to perform responsibly as young adults? Are we just going to throw another problem at the police and say, "Fix it"?

7

Are There Any Fallacies in the Reasoning?

Thus far, you have been working at taking the raw materials a writer or speaker gives you and assembling them into a meaningful overall structure. You have learned ways to remove the irrelevant parts from your pan as well as how to discover the "invisible glue" that holds the relevant parts together—that is, the assumptions. You have learned to do this by asking critical questions. let's briefly review these questions:

1. What are the issue and the conclusion?
2. What are the reasons?
3. What words or phrases are ambiguous?
4. What are the value conflicts and assumptions?
5. What are the descriptive assumptions?

Asking these questions should give you a clear understanding of the communicator's reasoning as well as a sense of where there might be strengths and weaknesses in the argument. Most remaining chapters focus on how well the structure holds up after being assembled. Your major question now is, "How acceptable is the conclusion?" You are now ready to make your central focus *evaluation. Remember:* The objective of critical reading and listening is to judge the acceptability or worth of conclusions.

While answering our first five questions has been a necessary beginning to the evaluation process, we now move to questions that require us to make judgments more directly and explicitly about the worth or the quality of the reasoning.

Your first step at this stage of the evaluation process is to examine the reasoning structure to determine whether the communicator has used a *questionable assumption* or has "tricked" you through either a *mistake in logic* or other forms of deceptive reasoning. You recall that the previous chapter focuses on finding and then thinking about the quality of assumptions. This chapter, on the other hand, highlights those reasoning "tricks" that we and others call *fallacies.*

Three common tricks are:

1. providing reasoning that requires *erroneous or incorrect assumptions,*
2. *distracting us* by making information seem relevant to the conclusion when it is not,
3. providing support for the conclusion that depends on the conclusion's already being true.

Let's see what a fallacy in reasoning looks like. In the fall of 1988, presidential candidate George Bush responded to the controversy surrounding whether the family of his running mate, Senator Dan Quayle, helped Quayle get into the Indian National Guard to avoid the Vietnam draft as follows:

> Dan Quayle served in the National Guard, signing up in a unit that had vacancies at the time and now he is under shrill partisan attack. . . . True, he didn't go to Vietnam, but his unit wasn't sent. But there's another truth; he did not go to Canada, he did not burn his draft card, and he damned sure didn't burn the American flag!

Note that Mr. Bush presented his "reason," and we have no reason to doubt it. But it was *not relevant* to the conclusion! The issue was whether Quayle's family helped him avoid the draft, not whether he is a patriot. As far as we know, Quayle also never bought foreign cars or talked back to his mother. But, these facts are also not relevant. We would have to supply an absurd assumption to "fill in the gap" between the reason and the conclusion. Rather than present a relevant reason, Mr. Bush appeals to our emotions and distracts us from the basic issue; he commits a fallacy in reasoning.

This chapter gives you practice in identifying such fallacies.

☞ *Critical Question:* **Are there any fallacies in the reasoning?**

Evaluating Assumptions

If you have been able to locate assumptions (see Chapters 5 and 6), especially descriptive assumptions, you already have a major skill in determining questionable assumptions and in finding fallacies. The more questionable the assumption, the less relevant the reasoning. Some reasoning will involve descriptive assumptions that you may reject. Some "reasons" will be so irrelevant to the conclusion that you would have to supply blatantly erroneous assumptions to provide a logical link. You should immediately reject such reasoning. Some reasoning will involve value assumptions, and you will have to use your own personal value preferences as a guide to evaluating them.

Caution: If you decide to keep a list of specific evaluation skills, don't forget the three we have already encountered:

1. Checking to see whether the communicator has satisfactorily clarified significant ambiguity.
2. Noting the failure of the communicator to justify value assumptions that are contrary to those you bring to the argument, and
3. Looking for questionable descriptive assumptions in the argument.

The chapters that touched on these skills focus on the important task of first identifying ambiguity and assumptions. Thus, as you study those chapters, it is quite easy to overlook the evaluation activities that are the eventual purpose of the discovery process.

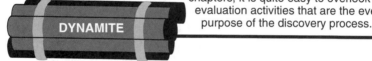

DYNAMITE

To demonstrate the process you should go through to evaluate assumptions, we will examine the quality of the reasoning in the following passage. We will begin by assembling the structure.

The question involved in this legislation is a critical one. It is not really a question of whether alcohol consumption is or is not detrimental to health. Rather, it is a question of whether Congress is willing to have the Federal Communications Commission make an arbitrary decision that prohibits alcohol advertising on radio and television. If we should permit the FCC to take this action in regard to alcohol, what is there to prevent them from deciding next year that candy is detrimental to the public health in that it causes obesity, tooth decay, and other health problems? What about milk and eggs? Milk and eggs are high in saturated animal fat and no doubt increase the cholesterol in the bloodstream, believed by many heart specialists to be a contributing factor in heart disease. Do we want the FCC to be able to prohibit the advertising of milk, eggs, butter, and ice cream on TV?

We all know that no action by the federal government, however drastic, can or will be effective in eliminating alcohol consumption completely. National prohibition of alcoholic beverages was attempted, but the Eighteenth Amendment, after only 14 years of stormy existence, was repealed by the Twenty-first.

CONCLUSION: *The FCC should not prohibit alcohol advertising on radio and television.*

REASONS: 1. *If we permit the FCC to prohibit advertising on radio and television, the FCC will soon prohibit many kinds of advertising, because many products present potential health hazards.*
2. *No action by the federal government can or will be effective in eliminating alcohol consumption completely. National prohibition of alcohol didn't work.*

First, the acceptability of the first reason depends on an underlying assumption that once we allow actions to be taken on the merits of one case, it will be impossible to stop actions on similar cases. We do not agree with this assumption, mainly because we believe that there are plenty of steps in our legal system to prevent such actions if they appear unjustified. Thus, we judge this reason to be unacceptable.

The credibility of the second reason is questionable because the link between the evidence and the reason relies on the suspect assumption that the outcome of national prohibition of alcohol is typical of most outcomes of federal government actions. Even if this reason were true, we disagree with an assumption linking the reason to the conclusion, the assumption that the major goal of prohibiting alcohol advertising on radio and television is to *eliminate alcohol consumption completely.* A more likely goal is to *reduce consumption.* Thus we judge this reason to be weakly supported because we believe the evidence used to support it is of questionable relevance.

As you search for errors in reasoning, *always keep the conclusion in mind;* then ask yourself, "What reasons would be adequate to support this position?" If there is a large difference between the reasons presented and what you believe to be relevant reasons, there is likely to be an error in reasoning. A further hint we can give you is that, typically, when individuals are claiming that one *action* is more desirable than another, relevant reasons will refer to the concrete advantages or disadvantages of adopting a particular position. When reasoning strays from advantages and disadvantages, be especially watchful for fallacies in reasoning.

Common Reasoning Fallacies

There are numerous common reasoning fallacies. Many are so common that they have been given fancy names. Fortunately, it is not necessary for you to be aware of all the common fallacies and their names to be able to locate them. If you ask yourself the right questions, you will be able to find reasoning fallacies—even if you can't name them. Thus, we have adopted the strategy of emphasizing self-questioning strategies, rather than asking you to memorize an extensive list of possible kinds of fallacies.

We are now going to take you through some exercises in discovering common fallacies. Once you know how to look, you will be able to find most fallacies. In Exercise A, do the following: First, identify the conclusion and reason. Second, determine whether the reason states a concrete advantage or a disadvantage. Third, identify any necessary assumption by asking yourself, "If the reason were true, what would one have to believe for it to logically support the conclusion, and what does one have to believe for the reason to be true?" Last, ask yourself, "Do these assumptions make sense?" If an obviously erroneous assumption is being made, you have found a fallacy in reasoning. And, that reasoning can be judged invalid.

Exercise A

Fluorine is the most toxic chemical on earth; it is so powerful in its corrosive effect that it is used to etch glass. The idea of putting that sort of chemical into our drinking water is just insane. Fluoridation is a menace to health.

Additionally, many medical associations are opposed to fluoridation. For instance, the Texas Medical Association declined to recommend it. However, it's not hard to explain why some doctors favor fluoridation. For instance, one of its leading advocates has been Dr. Danger, Dean and Research Professor of Nutrition at the State University Medical School. In the past six years, Dr. Danger received over $350,000 from the food processors, the refined-sugar interests, the soft-drink people, and the chemical and drug interests. Every true nutritionist knows that it is refined sweet soft drinks, and refined flour that are the basic causes of defective teeth. Is it any wonder that the processors of these foods are so active in helping the chemical interests to cover up for them?

As a first step in analyzing for fallacies, let's outline the argument.

CONCLUSION: *Drinking water should not be fluoridated.*

REASONS: 1. *Fluorine is the most dangerous toxic chemical on earth; it is so powerful in its corrosive effect that it is used to etch glass.*
2. *Many medical associates are opposed to fluoridation. The Texas Medical Association declined to recommend it.*
3. *Some doctors personally benefit by endorsing fluoridation. Dr. Danger received large sums of money from business groups during the time he endorsed fluoridation.*

In the first paragraph, the author tries to prove that fluoridation is very dangerous—a disadvantage. He does this by stating that fluorine is the most toxic chemical on earth; it is so powerful in its corrosive effect that it is used to etch glass. What erroneous assumptions are being made? First, note that the author used *fluorine* to prove something about *fluoridation*. A dictionary will quickly show you that fluorine is not the same as fluoride. The writer has *shifted words* on us. One cannot assume that fluorine and fluoride have the same effect; nor can one assume that any such chemicals when in diluted form will behave as they do in undiluted form. Thus, there is no proof here that fluoridation is dangerous—only that fluorine, in undiluted form, is dangerous. When someone propels us toward a conclusion by making a word or phrase *used in two distinctly different ways* in an argument appear to have the same meaning throughout, we call the reasoning the *fallacy of equivocation.*

Now, carefully examine the author's second argument, expressed in the first sentence of the second paragraph. What assumptions are being made? To prove that fluoridation is bad, he *appeals to authorities.* He thus moves away from pointing out factual advantages or disadvantages of fluoridation. A position is not bad just because authorities are against it. What is important in determining the relevance of such reasoning is the evidence that the authorities are using in making their judgment.

In addition, in this second argument the writer *shifts words* on us again. He argues that many medical associations "are opposed to" fluoridation and supports this with the fact that the Texas Medical Association "declined to recommend" it. Does *decline to recommend* mean the same as *oppose?* No—*oppose* implies definite disapproval; *decline to recommend* simply signifies an unwillingness to approve. Additionally, can we assume that the Texas Medical Association is representative of medical associations in general?

Consider the third argument, voiced in the last part of the second paragraph. Has the writer pointed out advantages or disadvantages of fluoridation? No. He has basically tried to prove that Dr. Danger is biased in his viewpoint. He has attacked Dr. Danger, who favors fluoridation. He has not proven anything about the benefits or dangers of fluoridation. Even if Dr. Danger is biased, his views on fluoridation may still be correct. The issue is whether or not fluoridation is desirable, not whether Dr. Danger is an ethical person. *One does not prove a point by attacking a person.* The assumption that because a person may have undesirable qualities, his ideas are therefore undesirable is clearly a bad assumption. Such an argument diverts attention from the issue. A good argument attacks ideas, not the person with the ideas. Attacking a person, rather than ideas, is frequently called an *ad hominem* argument.

Now, we will look at an argument favoring fluoridation.

Exercise B

Fluoridation is opposed by a crackpot, antiscientific minority. I do not believe that a minority ever has the right to keep the majority from getting what they want. In any city in which a majority of us want fluoridation, we should have it; that is the democratic way.

First, let's again keep the structure of the argument in mind as we search for errors. Also, let's once again ask whether the author has strayed from discussing the advantages and disadvantages of fluoridation.

Clearly, the author has not focused on the advantages and disadvantages. First, what do you think about the phrase "crackpot, antiscientific minority"? Obviously, he is giving his opponents a bad name. This practice of *name call-*

ing is unfortunately quite common. For this reason to support the conclusion, it must be assumed that if a group can be labeled with negative adjectives, then their ideas are erroneous. Wrong! Even if opponents of fluoridation deserve their bad name, it is still very possible that fluoridation *is* a bad thing, according to the *evidence*. Be wary of name calling!

What about the argument that we ought to do what the majority wants? Certainly it sounds very democratic. But what assurance do we have that the majority are basing their judgments on the *appropriate evidence?* What if there were evidence available that fluoridation caused cancer, but the majority continued to ignore the evidence? We think you get the point. There is no substitute for good evidence. Be wary of phrases like, "Most Americans agree that . . ." or "Everybody knows that. . . ." These phrases represent appeals to group-approved attitudes and are frequently referred to as *ad populum* arguments. Again, note that such arguments divert attention from the real issue.

Now let's examine some arguments related to another controversy: Should Congress approve a federally funded child-development program that would provide day-care centers for children?

Exercise C

I am against the government's child development program. First, I am interested in protecting the children of this country. They need to be protected from social planners and *self-righteous ideologues* who would disrupt the normal course of life and *tear* them from their mothers and families to make them *pawns* in a universal scheme designed to produce infinite happiness in 20 years. Children should grow up with their mothers, not with a series of caretakers and nurses' aides. What is at issue is whether parents shall continue to have the right to form the characters of their children, or whether the State with all its power should be given the tools and techniques for forming the young.

Let's again begin by outlining the argument.

CONCLUSION: *I am against the government's child-development program.*

REASONS: 1. *Our children need to be protected from social planners and self-righteous ideologues, who would disrupt the normal course of life and tear them from their families.*

2. *The parents, not the State, should have the right to form the characters of their children.*

As critical readers and listeners, we should be looking for specific facts about the program. Do you find any specifics in the first reason? No. The reason is saturated with undefined and emotionally loaded generalities. We have italicized several of these terms in the passage. Such terms will typically generate negative emotions, which the writer or speaker hopes readers and listeners will associate with the position he is attacking. Again, the writer is engaging in name calling. The use of emotionally charged negative terms serve to distract readers and listeners from the facts.

The writer has tricked us in another way. He states that the program will "tear them from their families and mothers," and the children will be "pawns in a universal scheme." Of course, nobody wants these things to happen to their children. However, the important question is whether *in fact* the bill will do these things. Not likely!

The writer is playing two common tricks on us. First, he is *appealing to our emotions* with his choice of words. Second, he has set up a position to attack which in fact does not exist, making it much easier to get us on his side. He has *extended* the opposition's position to an "easy-to-attack" position. The erroneous assumption in this case is that the position attacked is the same as the position actually presented in the legislation. The lesson for the critical thinker is: When someone attacks aspects of a position, always check to see if he is fairly representing the position. If he is not, you have located the *extension* error. The best way to check how fairly a position is being represented is to get the facts about all positions.

Let's now look closely at the second reason. The writer states that *either* parents shall have the right to form the characters of their children, *or else* the State should be given the decisive tools. For statements like this to be true, one must assume that there are only two choices. Are there? No! The writer has created a *false dilemma*. Isn't it possible for the child development program to exist and also for the family to have a significant influence on the child? Always be cautious when controversies are treated as if only two choices are possible; there are frequently more than two. When a writer or speaker oversimplifies an issue by stating only two choices, the error is referred to as an *either-or* error. To find *either-or* errors, be on the alert for phrases like the following:

either . . . or

the only alternative is

the two choices are

because A has not worked, *only* B will

Caution: Sometimes only two options exist. For example, a woman is either pregnant or she is not. So don't jump to the impression that a fallacy has occurred every time an argument tries to suggest that only two alternatives are possible. Rather, you should always wonder to yourself whether there is a third or fourth option that the communicator is either not noticing or does not want you to notice.

DYNAMITE

Let's shift to a different controversy: Should there be businesses that sell term papers to students?

What's wrong with buying term papers? Most students resort to buying them only because they realize that the system is rotten: the term paper itself has become a farce in the eyes of the students because they are required to go through the mechanical motions, month after month, of putting things down tediously on paper, writing correct sentences, organizing their paragraphs and ideas, thinking up arguments to use, and all those rituals—surely you aren't going to claim that that is education. Real education is ecstasy, the peak experience.[1]

Again, let's start by outlining the argument.

CONCLUSION: *Buying term papers is defensible.*

REASON: *Term paper rituals are not education; real education is ecstasy, the peak experience.*

The major reason given is "proven" by the "fact" that "real education is ecstasy, the peak experience." Sounds good—but what does it mean? The writer has tried to seduce the reader by using showy terms that have an emotional appeal. He has provided us with *glittering generalities,* hoping that we will not require a more precise or specific definition of the goals of education and of the appropriate behaviors for obtaining such goals. A position is not good or bad because we can associate it with a good or bad label or a smug phrase, *Good reasons provide specifics!*

Be especially on the lookout for glib phrases or pet slogans. Do you see why you should be wary of each of the following?

A woman's place is in the home. (All women?)

Nice guys finish last. (Always?)

Vote for our party—we are for peace and prosperity. (Who isn't?)

Human nature is unchangeable. (Always?)

Work is what made this country great. (The only thing?)

Moderation is everything. (Always?)

Further Diversions

Emotional language is one way that writers and speakers divert our attention from the issue. There is another very common diversionary device. Let's take a look.

I don't see how people can keep arguing that Japanese cars are a better buy than American cars. Why, just look at the recent performance of the Japanese economy compared to the American economy. They have experienced three years of economic decline, while we have enjoyed three years of relative prosperity.

[1]M. Beardsley, *Thinking Straight,* 4th ed. (Upper Saddle River, NJ: Prentice Hall, 1975), pp. 237–38.

What is the real issue? Which is a better car? Japanese or American? But if you are not careful you will get involved instead in the question of how the two economies are doing. The writer has diverted the reader's attention to another issue. When a writer or speaker does this, we can say that he has drawn a *red herring* across the trail of the argument. Red herring arguments are very common. Many of us are adept at these, as the following example illustrates:

If the daughter is successful, the issue will become whether the mother is picking on her daughter, not why the daughter was out late.

You should normally have no difficulty spotting red herrings as long as you keep the real issue in mind as well as the kind of evidence needed to resolve it.

Confusing "What Should Be" with "What Is"

Landlords should clean apartments before they rent them. By cleaning their rental properties, they will be giving their customers what any renter desires—a fresh apartment. Being fully aware of this moral obligation, I persuaded my brother to move to a rental unit in Colorado, even though he had never seen it. Now he's mad at me; the apartment was filthy when he arrived. I can't understand what happened.

Do you? The advice to move to Colorado to an unseen rental unit was based on an error in reasoning. That something *should be* true—that is, apartments should be clean when rented—in no way guarantees that what *is* true will conform to the prescription.

Another common illustration of this reasoning error occurs when discussing proposals for government regulation. For instance, someone might argue that regulating advertising for children's television programs is undesirable because parents *should* turn the channel or shut off the television if advertising is deceptive. Perhaps parents in a perfect world would behave in this fashion. Many parents, however, are too busy to monitor children's programming.

Whan a person reasons that someone *must be* telling the truth because people *should* tell the truth, he is committing a reasoning fallacy. This fallacy is often called *wishful thinking*. We would hope that what should be the case would guide our behavior. Yet many observations convince us that just because advertisers, politicians, and authors *should* not mislead us is no protection against their regularly misleading us. The world around us is a poor imitation of what the world should be like.

Here's a final example of wishful thinking that might sound familiar to you.

It can't be Thursday already; I haven't finished my paper yet.

Confusing Naming with Explaining

Another confusion is responsible for an error in reasoning that we often encounter when seeking explanations. To explain requires an analysis of why an event occurred. Explaining is demanding work that often tests the boundaries of what we know. When asked for an explanation, it's frequently tempting to hide our ignorance by labeling or naming what occurred. Then we assume that because we know the name, we know the cause.

We do so because the naming seduces us into believing we have identified something the person *has* that makes her act accordingly. For example, instead of specifying the complex set of situational factors that lead a person to manifest an angry emotion, we say the person *has* a "bad temper."

A couple of examples should be adequate to heighten your alertness to this conclusion:

1. In response to dad's heavy drinking, mom is asked by her adult daughter, "Why is dad behaving so strangely?" Mom replies, "He's having a midlife crisis."
2. A patient cries every time the counselor asks about his childhood. An intern who watched the counseling session asks the counselor, after the patient has left, "Why does he cry when you ask about his youth?" The counselor replies, "He's neurotic."

Perhaps in each case the respondent could have explained but was just in a hurry. But for whatever reasons, neither respondent satisfactorally explained what happened. For instance, the specifics of dad's genetic inheritance, job pressures, marital strife, and exercise habits would have provided the basis for explaining the heavy drinking. "A midlife crisis" is not only inadequate; it misleads. We think we know why dad is drinking heavily, but we don't.

Be especially alert for this error when people allege that they have discovered a cause for the behavior yet all they have provided is a different name for the behavior.

Searching for Perfect Solutions

1. I cannot support your request for a larger educational budget because there will still be illiterate people even if you received the extra funds.
2. Why try to restrict people's access to abortion clinics in the United States? Even if you were successful, a woman seeking an abortion could still fly to Europe to acquire an abortion.
3. Our city council decided not to hire an additional detective; crime would not cease just because we have another police officer on the payroll.

All three of these arguments take the same form.

A solution to X does not deserve our support unless it destroys the problem entirely. If we ever find a perfect solution, then we should adopt it.

In each case, the error in reasoning is the same. Just because part of a problem would remain after a solution is tried does not mean the solution is unwise. A partial solution may be vastly superior to no solution at all; it may make a contribution to solving the problem. It may move us a step closer to solving the problem completely. If we waited for perfect solutions to emerge, we would often find ourselves paralyzed, unable to act. A partial solution may be the best we can find.

Begging the Question

Sometimes a conclusion is supported by itself; only the words have been changed to fool the innocent! For example, to argue that dropping out of school is undesirable because it is bad is not to argue at all. The conclusion is "proven" by the conclusion (in different words). Such an argument *begs the question*, rather than answering it. Let's look at one that is a little less obvious.

Programmed-learning texts are clearly superior to traditional texts in learning effectiveness because it is highly advantageous for learning to have materials presented in a step-by-step fashion.

Again, the reason supporting the conclusion restates the conclusion in different words. By definition, programmed learning is a step-by-step procedure. The writer is arguing that such a procedure is good because it is good.

Let's examine one more example.

A comprehensive national health insurance plan is wasteful. Thus, passing such a bill would cause a great deal of harm. Because the bill would be so harmful, it is obviously a very wasteful bill.

How does the writer prove that passing the bill will be harmful? By claiming the bill is wasteful. How does he prove it is wasteful? By asserting the conclusion. Thus, the conclusion is used to support the reason that supports the conclusion. This is a special example of begging the question, commonly referred to as *circular reasoning.* The conclusion itself is used as proof for the assertion that is used to prove the conclusion. Thus, the conclusion has not been *proven;* it has been *assumed* in the proof.

Whenever a conclusion is *assumed* in the reasoning when it should have been proven, begging the question has occurred. When you outline the structure of an argument, check the reasons to be sure that they do not simply repeat the conclusion in different words and check to see that the conclusion is not used to prove the reasons. In case you are confused, let's illustrate with two examples, one argument that begs the question and one that does not.

(1) To allow the press to keep their sources confidential is very advantageous to the country because it increases the likelihood that individuals will report evidence against powerful people.

(2) To allow the press to keep their sources confidential is very advantageous to the country because it is highly conducive to the interests of the larger community that private individuals should have the privilege of providing information to the press without being identified.

Paragraph (2) begs the question by basically repeating the conclusion. It fails to point out what the specific advantages are, and simply repeats that confidentiality of sources is socially used.

Summary of Reasoning Errors

We have taken you through exercises that illustrate a number of ways in which reasoning may be erroneous. We have not listed all the ways, but we have given you a good start, and we will add more to your list in subsequent chapters. To find reasoning fallacies, keep in mind what kinds of reasons are good reasons— that is, the evidence and the moral principles *relevant to the issue.* Reasoning should be rejected whenever you have found mistaken assumptions, distractions, or support for the conclusion that already assumes the truth of the conclusion. Reasoning should be rejected when it:

attacks a person or a person's background, instead of the person's ideas,

presents a faulty dilemma,

oversimplifies,

diverts attention from the issue,

appeals to questionable authority,

confuses "what should be" with "what is,"

confuses naming with explaining,

reflects a search for perfect solutions, or

begs the question.

Reasoning should be approached cautiously when it appeals to group-approved attitudes and to authority. You should always ask, "Are there good reasons to consider such appeals as persuasive evidence?" A precautionary note is in order here: Do not *automatically* reject reasoning that relies on appeals to authority or group-approved attitudes. Carefully evaluate such reasoning. For example, if most physicians in the country choose to take up jogging, that information is important to consider in deciding whether jogging is beneficial. Some authorities do possess valuable information. Because of its importance as a source of evidence, we discuss appeals to authority in detail in the next chapter.

Writing and Reasoning

When you write essays, you necessarily engage in reasoning. If your purpose is to present a well-reasoned argument, in which you do not want to "trick" the reader into agreeing with you, then you will want to avoid committing reasoning fallacies. Awareness of possible errors committed by writers provides you with warnings to heed. You can avoid fallacies by checking your own assumptions very carefully, by remembering that most controversial issues require you to get specific about advantages and disadvantages, and by keeping a checklist handy of possible reasoning fallacies. A good source to help you become more familiar with reasoning fallacies is T. Edward Damer's book, *Attacking Faulty Reasoning.*

Practice Exercises

☞   *Critical Question: **Are there any fallacies in the reasoning?***

Try to identify fallacies in the reasoning in each of the three practice passages.

Passage 1

The surgeon general has overstepped his bounds by recommending that explicit sex education begin as early as third grade. It is obvious that he is yet another victim of the AIDS hysteria sweeping the nation. Unfortunately, his media-influenced announcement has given new life to those who favor explicit sex education— even to the detriment of the nation's children.

Sexuality has always been a topic of conversation reserved for the family. Only recently has sex education been forced on young children. The surgeon general's recommendation removes the role of the family entirely. It should be up to parents to explain sex to their children in a manner with which they are comfortable. Sex education exclusive of the family is stripped of values or any sense of morality, and should thus be discouraged. For years families have taken the responsibility of sex education, and that's the way it should remain.

Sex education in schools encourages experimentation. Kids are curious. Letting them in on the secret of sex at such a young age will promote blatant promiscuity. Frank discussions of sex are embarrassing for children, and they destroy the natural modesty of girls.

Passage 2

Students should be required to live in college dormitories because college administrators have determined that the benefits outweigh the costs. If students are required to live in dorms, they will be better students.

A most persuasive rationale for this conclusion is provided by remembering that college administrators are typically older than college students. Because they are older, they should be more knowledgeable about what is best for students. Recognizing this probability, we should support administrators' advice that student housing in college dormitories should be compulsory.

Passage 3

The National Endowment for the Arts is an inappropriate use of taxpayers' money. Government sponsorship of artistic enterprises is just wrong. While being wrong is reason enough to reject anything, government support for the arts has multiple additional drawbacks.

First, this method of helping the arts harms some artists. Imagine what it feels like to be an artist and to watch your competing artists receive a subsidy from the taxpayers, while you have to provide the sole support for *your* work. We should not support the arts until we figure out how to do it right.

Second, the arts should be supported by the community when it purchases art. Sure, you may respond that little art is bought by the public. Well, then, let's focus on that problem. Let's persuade people to buy more art, instead of using the government to purchase it for them.

Sample Responses

Passage 1

CONCLUSION: *Sex education should not be taught in schools.*

REASONS: *1. The report reflects hysteria.*
            2. It is the job of parents.
            3. Education encourages promiscuity.

The author begins the argument by attacking the surgeon general rather than the issue. She claims that the recommendation is a by-product of the AIDS hysteria rather than extensive research. Her suggestion that the surgeon general issues reports in reaction to hot topics in the media undermines his credibility and character and is therefore *ad hominem.*

Her second reason confuses "what is" with "what should be." Just because sex education *should be* up to the parents does not mean that they *will* provide education.

The third reason presents a false dilemma—either keep sex education out of the schools or face morally loose, value-free children. But isn't it possible to have morally loose children even when sex education is taking place in the home? Isn't it also a possibility that both parents and the schools can play a role in sex education? Might not education result in children who are prepared to handle the issue of sex in their lives rather than morally deficient delinquents?

Passage 2

First, we should note that we have a prescriptive argument. The issue is whether college students should be required to live in college dormitories. The first paragraph states two reasons for supporting such a requirement:

1. College administrators claim the benefits outweigh the costs.
2. Students will be better students if the requirement exists.

Neither reason is very convincing. What is the difference between saying the benefits of X outweigh the costs and saying college administrators favor X? Not much! Thus we can reword the reasons to say college administrators favor the requirement. In this form, we can see the reason as an appeal to authority. There does not appear to be any reason why we should rely on this particular appeal.

The second reason claims that the requirement will make students better. A rewording of the issue in the form of the question might be, would college students be "better" if required to live in college dormitories? It is begging the question to respond that the answer is "yes" because they would be better. We have not advanced the conversation at all.

The third reason, provided in the second paragraph, represents a confusion between what should be and what is.

3. Because administrators should be more knowledgeable about students' welfare, they are.

If one accepted the third reason, one would support the requirement if administrators do. Many things should be true, but reality rarely conforms to these prescriptions on our part.

After looking critically at the three reasons and the conclusion, we cannot support the reasoning. We could be convinced, perhaps, but not by what was provided in this practice passage.

Passage 3

CONCLUSION: *We should oppose the use of tax money to support the National Endowment for the Arts.*

REASONS: 1. *Taxpayer support for the arts is wrong.*
2. *Until we find a method of support for the arts that hurts no artists, we should do nothing to support artists.*
3. *The arts should be supported by consumer purchases.*

The first reason begs the question. Why should the taxpayers oppose support for the National Endowment for the Arts? The writer answers: because it is wrong. So we are being urged to see as wrong something that is wrong because it is declared to be wrong. But we are left to wonder, what is so wrong about it?

The second reason asks us to wait until we have found a perfect solution before we try to correct a problem. This fallacy would require us to resist any and all solutions for it is hard to imagine any solution for any problem that would not have at least one drawback. Any solution to the lack of support for the arts will harm some artist somewhere.

Finally, the third reason confuses "what should be" with "what is." It is always easy to imagine a world that does not exist and then compare this better world to a proposed solution. The proposed solution will always lose in such a comparison. But we must find solutions in this world. If consumers will not buy art in optimal amounts, then it does us little good to oppose subsidies to the arts while waiting for consumer behavior to change in a radical fashion.

Passage 4 (Self-Examination)

Higher tuition suggests superior education. These schools called superior by books that rate the quality of colleges and universities are exactly those schools that cost the most to attend. Consequently, you must either pay higher tuition or receive an inferior education.

Higher tuition permits higher salaries for professors. If professors are not kept happy by higher salaries, the quality of the teaching will suffer. The American Federation of Teachers points out that the contented faculty member is repeatedly the same one who is rated superior by supervisors.

The point is that students have a vested interest in paying higher tuition. Those students who gripe about tuition are simply uninformed. We all know that you get what you pay for.

8

How Good Is the Evidence: Intuition, Appeals to Authority, and Testimonials?

Which of us can claim to know how to stop one person from killing another?

Wardens can. Those who manage our prisons regularly remind us that severity of penalty crosses the mind of many potential murderers.

In the last chapter you made major inroads into the process of evaluating persuasive communications by learning how to detect some fallacies in reasoning. In our next few chapters, we continue our focus on evaluation as we learn to ask critical questions about a specific part of the reasoning structure: claims about the "facts." Let's see what such claims look like.

Eating oat bran reduces the risk of cancer.

Infidelity is rampant in the United States; over 40 percent of married men admit to having affairs.

The fact of the matter is the Japanese are building better cars.

College campuses are not safe; *Time* magazine reports that on-campus assaults have increased by 10 percent over the last three years.

What do we make of these claims? Are they legitimate? Most reasoning includes claims such as these. In this chapter, we begin the process of evaluating such claims.

☞   *Critical Question:* **How good is the evidence: intuition, appeals to authority, and testimonials?**

The Need for Evidence

Almost all reasoning we encounter includes beliefs about the way the world is, was, or is going to be that the communicator wants us to accept as "facts." These beliefs can be conclusions, reasons, or assumptions. We can refer to such beliefs as *factual claims.*

The first question, you should ask about a factual claims is, *"Why should I believe it?"*

Your next question is, *"Does the claim need evidence to support it?"*

If it does, and if there is no evidence, the claim is a *mere assertion.* You should seriously question the dependability of mere assertions!

If there *is* evidence, your next question is, *"How good is the evidence?"*

To evaluate reasoning, we need to remember that some factual claims can be counted on more than others. For example, you probably feel quite certain that the claim "most United States senators are men" is true, but less certain that the assertion "eating oat bran reduces the risk of heart attacks" is true.

Because it is extremely difficult, if not impossible, to establish the *absolute* truth or falsity of most claims, rather than ask whether they are *true,* we prefer to ask whether they are *dependable.* In essence, we want to ask, *"Can we count on such beliefs?"* The greater the quality and quantity of evidence supporting a claim, the more we can *depend on* it, and the more we can call the claim a *"fact."*

For example, abundant evidence exists that Bill Clinton defeated Bob Dole in the 1996 presidential election. Thus, we can treat the belief "Bill Clinton defeated Bob Dole" as a fact. On the other hand, there is much conflicting evidence for the belief "homosexuality is inherited." We thus can't treat this belief as a fact. The major difference between claims that are *opinions* and those that are *facts* is the present state of the relevant evidence. The more support evidence provides for a belief, the more "factual" the belief becomes

Before we judge the persuasiveness of a communication, we need to know which factual claims are most dependable. How do we do this? We ask questions like the following:

What is your proof?	How do you know that's true?
Where's the evidence?	Why do you believe that?
Are you sure that's true?	Can you prove it?

You will be well on your way to being among the best critical thinkers when you develop the habit of regularly asking these questions. They require those making arguments to be responsible by revealing the basis for their arguments. Anyone with an argument that you should consider will not hesitate to answer these questions. They know they have substantial support for their claims and, consequently, will want to share their evidence in the hope that you will learn to share their conclusions.

When we regularly ask these questions, we notice that for many beliefs there is insufficient evidence to support or to refute them. For example, much evidence supports the assertion that taking an aspirin every other day reduces the risk of heart attack, although some other evidence disputes it. In such cases, we need to make judgments about where the *preponderance of evidence* lies as we decide on the dependability of the factual claim.

Making such judgments requires us to ask the important question, *"How good is the evidence?"* The next three chapters focus on questions we need to ask to decide how well communicators have supported their factual claims. The more dependable the factual claims, the more persuasive the communications should be.

> **Caution:** One possible confusion at this stage is between fact and opinions. While the latter is a naked statement of belief, a fact is quite different. A fact is a statement about the world that has passed through various levels of examination, each attempting to verify or refute what is being called factual. While any particular fact might be unreliable for all sorts of reasons, facts as a category are much more reliable than opinions because they have been examined and tested by others before being called facts.
>
> **DYNAMITE**

Locating Factual Claims

We encounter factual claims as (a) *descriptive conclusions,* (b) *reasons* used to support either descriptive or prescriptive conclusions, or (c) as *assumptions.* Let's examine an example of each within brief arguments.

> (a) *Dieting may contribute to the development of eating disorders.* Researchers studied the dieting histories and the severity of binge-eating episodes among 111 women enrolled in a treatment program for eating disorders and found that 60 percent of the women reported that their first eating binge followed their initial dieting attempts.

Note that "dieting may contribute to the development of eating disorders" is a factual claim that is a descriptive conclusion supported by research evidence. In this case, we want to ask, "Is that conclusion—a factual claim—justified by the evidence?"

(b) We should decrease the sizes of classes in our universities. *Large classes are leading to greater student alienation,* according to recent government statistics.

Note that the factual claim here is the generalization that "large classes are leading to greater student alienation," and it functions as a reason supporting a prescriptive conclusion. In this case, we want to ask, "Is that reason—a factual claim—justified by the evidence?"

(c) We cannot afford any more immigrants in this country. The largest number of immigrants—over 6.5 million—have settled in California and cost California alone an estimated $3 billion annually in extra health care, schooling, and other public services. (Unstated descriptive assumption: *The positive impact of immigrants on the economy, through such benefits as creating new jobs and paying taxes, is significantly less than the cost.*)

Note that this factual claim is a descriptive assumption, which may or may not be dependable. Before we believe the assumption, and thus the reason, we want to ask, "How well is it backed up by evidence?"

Sources of Evidence

When should we judge a factual claim as dependable? There are three instances in which we will be inclined to agree with a factual claim:

1. when the claim appears to be undisputed common knowledge, such as the claim "weight lifting increases muscular body mass."
2. when the claim is the conclusion of a well-reasoned argument.
3. when the claim is adequately supported by solid evidence in the same communication or by other evidence that we know.

Our concern in this chapter is the third instance. Determining whether it is satisfied requires us to ask, "How good is the evidence?" To answer this question, we must first ask, "What do we mean by *evidence?*"

We define *evidence* as specific information in the form of research findings, examples, statistics, metaphors, and analogies, which is used to support the dependability of a factual claim (see Chapter 3).

The quality of evidence depends on its source. Thus, to evaluate evidence, we first need to ask, "What is its source? Knowing the source tells us what questions we should ask.

Major sources of evidence include

-   intuition
-   authorities and testimonials
-   personal experience

- personal observations
- case studies and examples
- research studies
- analogies

When used appropriately, each kind of evidence can be "good evidence." It can help support an author's claim. Like a gold prospector closely examining the gravel in his pan for potentially high-quality ore, we must closely examine the evidence to determine its quality. We want to know, "Does an author's evidence provide dependable supporter for her claim?" Thus, we begin to evaluate evidence by asking, *"How good is the evidence?"*

In this chapter and the next one, we examine what kinds of questions we can ask of each source to help us decide. Sources examined in this chapter are intuition, authority, and testimonials.

Intuition As a Source of Evidence

When we use intuition to support a claim, we rely on "common sense," or on our "gut feelings," or on hunches. When a communicator supports a claim by saying "common sense tells us," or "I just know that it's true," he is using intuition as his evidence.

A major problem with intuition is that it is private; others have no way to judge its dependability. Thus, when intuitive beliefs differ, which is often the case, how do we decide which ones to believe? Consequently, we must be very wary of claims backed up only by intuition.

However, sometimes communicators' "intuition" may in fact be relying on some other kind of evidence, such as extensive relevant personal experiences and readings. For example, when an experienced pilot has an intuition that the plane doesn't feel right as it taxis for takeoff, we might be quite supportive of further safety checks of the plane prior to takeoff. Sometimes "hunches" are not blind. As critical thinkers, we would want to find out whether claims relying on intuition have any other kinds of evidential support.

Authority As a Source of Evidence

A speaker makes the claim that Japanese cars are superior to American cars. When we ask him how he knows, he says, *"Consumer Reports* says so, and also an article I saw in *The New York Times* last week claimed that the Japanese make better cars."

The speaker has defended his claim by appealing to authority—sources that are supposed to know more than most of us about a given topic—so-called experts. When communicators appeal to authorities or experts, they appeal to people who they believe are in a position to have access to certain facts and to have special qualifications for drawing conclusions from the facts. You encounter appeals to many forms of authority on a daily basis.

> Movie reviewers: "One of the ten best movies of the year." Valerie Viewer, *Toledo Gazette.*
>
> Organizations: "The American Medical Association supports this position."
>
> Researchers: "Studies show . . ."
>
> Relatives: "My grandfather says . . ."
>
> Religion: "The Koran says . . ."
>
> Magazines: "According to *Newsweek* . . ."
>
> College professors: "The appropriate interpretation of Plato is . . ."
>
> Expert witnesses: "It is my belief that the defendant . . ."

You can easily add to our list. It should be obvious that some appeals to authority should be taken much more seriously as evidence than others. Why? Because some authorities are much more careful in giving an opinion than others. For example, *Newsweek* and *Time* are much more likely to carefully evaluate the available evidence prior to stating an opinion than is *The National Enquirer.* Our relatives are much less likely to have systematically evaluated a political candidate than are editorial writers for major newspapers.

You should remember that for many reasons, *authorities are often wrong.* Also, they often disagree.

The following examples, taken from *The Experts Speak,* are clear reminders of the fallibility of expert opinion.

> "It is once and for all clear . . . that the earth is in the middle of the world and all weights move towards it." Ptolemy (Alexandrian astronomer and geographer), *The Almagest,* second century A.D.

> "Erection is chiefly caused by scuraum, eringoes, cresses, crymon, parsnips, artichokes, turnips, asparagus, candied ginger, acorns bruised to powder and drank in muscadel, scallion, seashell fish, etc." Aristotle (Greek philosopher), *The Masterpiece,* fourth century B.C.

> "Nature intended women to be our slaves . . . They are our property . . . They belong to us, just as a tree that bears fruit belongs to a gardener. What a mad idea to demand equality for women! . . . Women are nothing but machines for producing children." Napoleon Bonaparte (1769–1821).

> "Video won't be able to hold onto any market it captures after the first six months. People will soon get tired of staring at a plywood box every night." Darryl F. Zanuck (Head of Twentieth Century Fox Studios), ca. 1946.

> "If excessive smoking actually plays a role in the production of lung cancer, it seems to be a minor one." Dr. W. C. Heuper (National Cancer Institute), quoted in *The New York Times,* April 14, 1954.

These quotes should remind us that we need to ask critical questions when communicators appeal to authority. We need to ask, *"Why should we believe this authority?"* More specifically, we should ask the following questions of authorities.

How much expertise or training does the authority have on the subject about which he is communicating? For example, is this a topic the person has studied for a long time? Or, has the person had extensive experience related to the topic?

Was the authority in a position to have especially good access to pertinent facts? For example, was she a firsthand observer of the events about which she makes claims? Or, has a newspaper reporter, for example, actually witnessed an event, or has she merely relied upon reports from others? If the authority is not a firsthand observer, whose claims is she repeating? Why should we rely on those claims? In general, you should be more impressed by *primary sources*—or direct observers—than by *secondary sources,* those who are relying on others for their evidence. *Time* and *Newsweek,* for example, are secondary sources, while research journals such as the *Journal of the American Medical Association* are primary sources.

Is there good reason to believe that the authority is relatively free of distorting influences? Among the factors that can influence how evidence is reported are personal needs, prior expectations, general beliefs, attitudes, values, theories, and ideologies. These can subconsciously or deliberately affect how evidence is presented. For example, if a general in the military is asked whether cuts in military spending are bad for the military, he may answer "yes" and give a number of good reasons. He may be giving an unbiased view of the situation. Because of his position, however, we would want to be concerned about the possibility that he has sought out reasons to justify his own biases.

By bias and prejudice, we mean possessing a strong personal feeling about the goodness or badness of something, such that it interferes with our ability to evaluate it fairly. Because many factors bias us in virtually all our judgments, we cannot expect any authority to be *totally* unbiased. We can, however, expect less bias from some authorities than from others and try to determine such bias by seeking information about the authority's personal interest in the topic under discussion. For example, we want to be especially wary if an authority stands to benefit financially from the actions she advocates.

Because an authority can have a personal interest in an issue and still make dependable claims, we should not reject a claim simply because we suspect that the authority's personal interests may interfere with her fairness. One helpful step we can take is to check to see whether authorities with diverse attitudes, prior expectations, values, and interests agree. Thus we need to ask the questions: "Has the authority developed a reputation for frequently making dependable claims? Have we been able to rely on this authority in the past?"

You will want to be especially concerned about the quality of authorities when you encounter factual claims on the Internet. There, virtually everyone becomes an "authority," because people are free to claim whatever they wish, and there is no built-in process to evaluate such claims. It is clearly a "buyer beware" situation!

When evaluating authority as a source of evidence, you need to remember that none of the following characteristics guarantees that an authority will be right:

- *Age.* We are not necessarily good authorities simply because we have gotten older.
- *Being in print.* It is as easy to make false claims in writing as it is by word of mouth.
- *Status.* Movie and television stars, sports figures, news anchors, doctors, businessmen, political pundits, and people with lots of money have high status. Being in this position doesn't mean they have special knowledge related to claims they make. It makes good sense to pay a lot of attention to Michael Jordan's claims about basketball strategy; it makes less sense to rely on his ideas about shoes he is promoting for financial gain, or his view about U.S. political strategy in the Middle East.

Personal Testimonials As a Source of Evidence

"You should see Dr. Feelgood for your surgery. He did a great job on my shoulder."

"Smoothest ride I have ever had in a car. You should consider buying one."

"In only six weeks, I lost ten pounds, using Lesflab. I highly recommend it to you."

"She's a great teacher. You should take her class."

As you well know from watching commercials, reading ads for movies, and talking to your friends, communicators often try to convince you of a point by using a particular kind of appeal to authority; they quote particular persons as saying that a given idea or product is good or bad, based upon their personal experiences. Such quoted statements serve as *personal testimonials.*

How helpful is such evidence? Usually, it is not very helpful at all. In most cases we should pay little attention to personal testimonials until we find out much more about the expertise, interests, values, and biases behind them. We should be especially wary of each of the following problems with testimonials:

- *Selectivity.* People's experiences differ greatly. Those trying to persuade us have usually carefully selected the testimony they use. We should always ask the question, "What was the experience like for those whom we have *not* heard from?"
- *Personal interest.* Many testimonials, such as those used for books, movies, and television products come from people who have something to gain from their testimony. For example, authors will sometimes provide positive testimonials for others, expecting a return of the favor when their book is reviewed. Thus, we need to ask, "Does the person providing the tes-

timony have a relationship with what she is advocating such that we can expect a strong bias in her testimony?"

- *Omitted information.* Testimonials rarely provide sufficient information about the basis for the judgment. For example, when a friend of yours raves about a teacher, you would want to ask why he was so impressed. Our standards may differ from the standards of those giving the testimony. We often have too little information to decide whether we should treat such claims seriously.

Dangers of Appealing to Personal Experience As Evidence

Because personal experiences are very vivid in our memories, we often rely on them, or on personal experiences reported to us by friends or relatives, as evidence to support a belief. For example, you might have a really frustrating experience with a lawyer because she greatly overcharges you for her services, leading you to believe that most lawyers overcharge. While the generalization about lawyers may or may not be true, relying on such experiences as the basis for a general belief is a bad mistake! That is because a single personal experience, or even an accumulation of personal experiences, is not enough to give you a *representative* sample of experiences. A single striking experience or several such experiences can demonstrate that certain outcomes are *possible;* for example, you may have met several people who smoked three packs of cigarettes a day and lived to the age of 90. Such experiences, however, can't demonstrate that such outcomes are *typical.*

Caution: Beware of the individual who says, "My experience proves . . ." or "I can disprove all that because of an experience I had . . . ." The critical thinker is always skeptical of experiences, subjects them to critical analysis, and determines whether they have been adequately confirmed by other sources of evidence, such as a research study.

DYNAMITE

Summary

In this chapter, we have focused on the evaluation of several kinds of evidence used to support factual claims: intuition, appeals to authorities, and personal testimonials. Such evidence must be relied on with caution. We have provided you with some questions you should ask to determine whether such evidence is *good evidence.* In the next chapter, we discuss other kinds of evidence, as we continue to ask the question, *"How good is the evidence?"*

Practice Exercises

☞   *Critical Question:* **How good is the evidence: intuition, appeals to authority, and testimonials?**

Evaluate the evidence in the following three passages.

Passage 1

While educational costs skyrocket, students are getting less and less for their money. They are paying $20,000 a year for their education; but they are not getting the teaching they think they are paying for. Professors are putting their time and energy into research, not into teaching. Consider the following comments from students attending a major research university.

Sandra W., sophomore English major: "You sit in classes with three hundred other students while you listen to a graduate student who can't even speak English."

Lori L., junior psychology major and honors student: "I've been in college over three years, and I still haven't had any one-to-one contact with a professor."

John M., freshman philosophy major: "It's impossible to find professors when you need them. One professor of mine was on campus only one day a week."

Passage 2

Are silicone breast implants dangerous? It looks as if women who have had such surgery can again feel safe. In a recent interview, Dr. Walter Newbody, a nationally known West Coast plastic surgeon, stated that implants are perfectly safe. He reports that in 10 years of performing silicone-gel implants, he has noted no serious problems resulting from the implants. Furthermore, the Southwestern Association of Plastic Surgery has declared in a recent publication that implants do not trigger autoimmune disorders, despite the claims of some physicians.

Passage 3

"What asylum doctor has not had his own attack of madness by dint of continual association with madmen? . . . But before that, what obscure inclination, what dreadful fascination had made him choose that subject?" (quoted from Marcel Proust).

"I think that my parents were crazy and I think that somehow, being psychiatrists kept them in line. They used it as a protection. They're both quite crazy, but their jobs gave them a really good cover." (Quote taken from a child of psychiatrists.)

It is commonplace that psychotherapists are crazy, and that this is probably what led them to their jobs. "What still strikes me," one woman I interviewed said, "is I'll go to a party in New York, and inevitably the craziest person there is a psychiatrist. I mean the person who is literally doing childish, antisocial things, and making a fool of himself. A president of the American Academy of Psychotherapists provides additional evidence in an address to the members of his organization, "When I first visited a national psychiatric convention, in 1943, I was dismayed to find the greatest collection of oddballs, Christ beards, and psychotics that I had ever seen outside a hospital. The "helping professions," notably psychotherapy, appear to attract more than their share of the emotionally unstable."[1]

Sample Responses

Passage 1

CONCLUSION: *Students at major research universities are not getting their money's worth.*

REASON: *Three students state dissatisfaction with the teaching they are receiving.*

Although the general conclusion may or may not be accurate, we should not rely on these testimonials as good "proof." This passage illustrates well the weaknesses of testimony as evidence. How typical are these "horror stories"? Would other students have raved about their teachers? How were the interviews conducted? Is the author's selection of interview comments biased? Did the students know what the interviewer was trying to prove and thus try to please the interviewer? Before we conclude that students were being cheated in their education, we would want much better evidence than just a few testimonials. What the testimonials do tell us, however, is that it is *possible* for students to have bad experiences with teachers at this university.

Passage 2

CONCLUSION: *Breast implants are safe.*

REASON: *A surgeon and a state professional organization claim implants are safe.*

How much should we depend on these appeals to authority? Not much. First, both authorities are likely to be very biased. They stand to gain financially by making safety claims. Dr. Newbody's testimony is especially suspect because it is based on his experiences only. He has probably not sought out evidence of failures. We might pay more attention to the claims of the state professional organization if it were to provide us with the research information on which its claim is based.

Passage 3

CONCLUSION: *The helping professions, especially psychotherapy, attract more than their share of emotionally unstable people.*

REASONS: 1. *A famous novelist and essayist raises suspicions about motives for choosing the profession of psychotherapy.*
2. *A child testifies her parents were crazy psychiatrists.*
3. *Unknown woman testifies she met a crazy psychiatrist at a party.*
4. *Claim by the president of the American Academy of Psychotherapists that psychotherapists are driven by their own emotional hunger.*

[1]Adapted from T. Maeder, "Wounded Healers," *Atlantic Monthly,* January 1989, pp. 37–38.

Has this passage convinced you that psychotherapists are crazier than the rest of us? They may or may not be, but the evidence presented here has not proven it. The "reasons" are a mix of personal testimonials (2 and 3), and appeals to authority (1 and 4). Because Proust was well-known for his insightful observations of human emotions and subconscious processes, we should probably pay some attention to the fact that he has raised this question and wonder, "Has he got something there?" The quote thus suggests the possibility of a craziness but gives no concrete evidence to support its presence. The personal testimonials are highly *selective*. How many people have met psychotherapists who do *not* seem crazy?

We should pay more attention to a president of a highly relevant association, the American Academy of Psychotherapists, than to the average person, because the association president has had extensive experience with psychotherapists. However, he is likely to be a biased observer and has appealed to a single biased experience to prove his point. For example, we cannot assume that psychotherapists who attended this convention are typical of all psychotherapists. Also, he seems to rely primarily on intuition, when he states, "Psychotherapists are those of us who are driven by our own emotional hunger."

This author has not strongly supported his factual claim.

Passage 4 (Self-Examination)

The popularity of modern movies, with their graphic violence on full display, has a negative impact on our public health. The disgusting scenes in a large number of popular movies desensitizes us to crime. But even more importantly, the common link between violence and premarital sex in movies contributes to an acceptance of a casual attitude towards sex in impressionable audiences.

Professor James McCarthy has concluded, for instance, "The movie industry is corrupt; they care little about the quality of our civilization as they pursue their mansions and luxury vacations. Their motto is: If it sells, it's good. Just last week I had to counsel one of my students who claimed that what looked so fun in the movies had turned into the nightmare of an unwanted pregnancy for her."

In addition, statistics reveal that 1 in 12 teenagers will be pregnant before they leave high school. Before there were movies with nudity in them, one almost never heard of teen mothers. I know that I was not tempted in my youth by such irresponsible movies; as a consequence, the life I now enjoy is filled with satisfaction.

9

How Good Is the Evidence: Personal Observation, Case Studies, Research Studies, and Analogies?

In this chapter, we continue our evaluation of evidence. We focus on four common sources of evidence: personal observation, case studies, research studies, and analogies. We need to question each of these as we encounter them as evidence.

☞   *Critical Question:* **How good is the evidence: personal observation, case studies, research studies, and analogies?**

Personal Observation

One valuable type of evidence is personal observation, which forms the basis for much scientific research. We feel confident of something we actually *see*. Thus, we highly value eyewitness testimony as evidence. A difficulty with personal observation, however, is the tendency to see or hear what we wish to see or hear, selecting and remembering those aspects of an experience that are most consistent with our previous experience and background. Let's examine two excerpts of reports on the same event: the firing of the first shot at the Battle of Lexington.

First, some context: In the spring of 1775, neither the British nor the colonists wanted to be the aggressor in any conflict. No matter what the precautions on either side, shots were fired at Lexington on the morning of April 19, 1775. Men were wounded and some men died. Who was responsible? Certainly, neither side wanted to accept the blame. The following statements were made by men who were there. They are firsthand, eyewitness accounts. Thomas Fessenden, a colonial onlooker, gave this sworn testimony to the justices of the peace:

Lexington, April 23, 1775

I, Thomas Fessenden, of lawful age, testify and declare, that being in a pasture near the meeting-house at said Lexington, on Wednesday, last, at about half an hour before sunrise, . . . I saw three officers on horseback advance to the front of said Regulars, when one of them being within six rods of the said Militia, cried out, "Disperse, you rebels, immediately"; on which he brandished his sword over his head three times; meanwhile the second officer, who was about two rods behind him, fired a pistol pointed at said Militia, and the Regulars kept huzzaing till he had finished brandishing his sword, and when he had thus finished brandishing his sword, he pointed it down towards said Militia, and immediately the said Regulars fired a volley at the Militia and then I ran off, as fast as I could, while they continued firing till I got out of their reach. I further testify, that as soon as ever the officer cried "Disperse, you rebels," the said Company of Militia dispersed every way as fast as they could, and while they were dispersing the Regulars kept firing at them incessantly, and further saith not.

Thomas Fessenden

The following version came from the personal diary of a young British officer, Lieutenant John Barker:

19th. At 2 o'clock we began our March by wading through a very long ford up to our Middles: after going a few miles we took 3 or 4 People who were going off to give intelligence; about 5 miles on this side of a Town called Lexington, which lay in our road, we heard there were some hundreds of People collected together intending to oppose us and stop our going on; at 5 o'clock we arrived there, and saw a number of People, I believe between 2 and 300, formed in a Common in the middle of the Town; we still continued advancing, keeping prepared against an attack tho' without intending to attack them; but on our coming near them they fired one or two shots, upon which our Men without any orders, rushed in upon them, fired and put 'em to flight; several of them were killed, we cou'd not tell how many, because they were got behind Walls and into the Woods; We had a Man of the 10th light Infantry wounded, nobody else hurt. We then formed on the Common, but with some difficulty, the Men were so wild they cou'd hear no orders; we waited a considerable time there, and at length proceeded on our way to - Concord. . . .

The preceding example should serve to remind us that observers, unlike certain mirrors, do not give us "pure" observations. What we "see" and report is "filtered" through a set of values, biases, attitudes, and expectations.

Thus, while personal observations can often be valuable sources of evidence, we need to recognize that they are not unbiased "mirrors of reality."

Case Studies As Sources of Evidence

Often, communicators will rely on a particular kind of observational evidence: case studies. We define a *case study* as a systematic observation of a single individual or event. For example, Sigmund Freud supported many beliefs about people by carefully observing and reporting on individual cases. Also, feminists have relied on case studies to support beliefs about how women are treated in the work force or in literature. Journalists often begin persuasive essays with vivid descriptions of cases. For example, one way to argue that stricter gun-control laws are needed is to provide vivid case studies of innocent people who have been killed by guns.

Vivid case studies should be viewed more as *striking examples* than as proof. Like personal experiences, they demonstrate *possibilities*. Thus, you must be especially wary of their use as evidence. Dramatic case studies are very concrete and easy to visualize, but such studies frequently blind us to relevant research evidence. For example, a detailed description of an obese welfare mother who has been irresponsible, has lived on welfare for 10 years, has lived with multiple husbands, and has had children by each of them may lead you to ignore the more relevant statistical data that only 10 percent of welfare recipients remain on welfare rolls for four years or longer.

Be wary of striking examples as proof!

Although examples will be consistent with a conclusion, do not let that consistency fool you. Always ask yourself: "Is the example typical?" "Are there powerful counterexamples?" "Are there biases in how the example is exported?"

Research Studies As a Source of Evidence

"Studies show . . ."

"Research investigators have found . . ."

"A recent report in the *New England Journal of Medicine* reports . . ."

One form of authority that relies a great deal on observation and often carries special weight is the research study: usually a systematic *collection of observations* by people trained to do scientific research. How dependable are research findings? Like appeals to any authority, we can't tell about the dependability of research findings until we ask lots of questions.

Society has turned to the scientific method as an important guide for determining the facts because the relationships among events in our world are very complex, and because humans are fallible in their observations and theories about these events. The scientific method attempts to avoid many of the built-in biases in our observations of the world and in our intuition and common sense.

What is special about the scientific method? Above all, it seeks information in the form of *publicly verifiable data*—that is, data obtained under conditions such that other qualified people can make similar observations and obtain the same results. A second major characteristic of scientific method is *control*—that is, minimizing extraneous factors that might affect the accuracy and interpretation of generalizations.

For example, if bias in observations may be a major problem, researchers might try to control this by using multiple observers. Physical scientists frequently maximize control by studying problems in the laboratory. When researchers do experiments, they try to minimize extraneous factors. Unfortunately, control is usually more difficult in the social world than in the physical world; thus it is very difficult to successfully apply the scientific method to many questions about complex human behavior.

Precision in language is a third major component of the scientific method. Our concepts are often confusing, obscure, and ambiguous. Scientific method tries to be precise and consistent in its use of language.

While there is much more to science than we can discuss here, we want you to keep in mind that scientific research, when conducted well, is one of our best sources of evidence because it emphasizes verifiability, control, and precision.

Unfortunately, the fact that research has been applied to a problem does not necessarily mean that the research evidence is dependable evidence. Like appeals to any source, appeals to research evidence must be approached with caution. Also, some questions, particularly those that focus on human behavior, can be answered only tentatively even with the best of evidence. Thus, there are a number of important questions we want to ask about research studies before we decide how much we want to depend on their evidence.

When communicators appeal to research as a source of evidence, you should remember the following:

1. Research varies greatly in *quality;* we should rely more on some research studies than others. There is well-done research and there is poorly done research, and we should rely more on the former. Because the research process is so complex and subject to so many external influences, even those well-trained in research practices sometimes conduct flawed research studies; and being published in a scientific journal does not guarantee that a research study is not flawed in important ways.

2. Research findings often contradict one another. Thus, *single* research studies presented out of the context of the family of research studies that

investigate the question often provide misleading conclusions. Research findings that most deserve our attention are those that have been repeated by more than one researcher or group of researchers.

3. Research findings *do not prove* conclusions. At best, they *support* conclusions. Research findings do not speak for themselves! Researchers must always *interpret* the meaning of their findings, and all findings can be interpreted in more than one way. Thus, researchers' conclusions should not be treated as demonstrated "truths." When you encounter statements such as "research findings show . . ." you should retranslate them into "researchers interpret their research findings as showing . . ."

4. Like all of us, researchers have expectations, attitudes, values, and needs that bias the questions they ask, the way they conduct their research, and the way they interpret their research findings. Despite its best efforts to avoid bias, science is not a neutral, value-free, totally objective enterprise. For example, scientists often have an emotional investment in a particular hypothesis. Like all fallible human beings, they may find it difficult to objectively treat data that conflict with that hypothesis. A major strength of scientific research is that it tries to make public its procedures and results so that others can judge the merit of the research and try to replicate it. However, regardless of how objective a scientific report may seem, important subjective elements are always involved.

5. Speakers and writers often distort or simplify research conclusions. Major discrepancies may occur between the conclusion merited by the original research and the use of the evidence to support a communicator's beliefs. For example, researchers may carefully qualify their own conclusions in their original research report only to have the conclusions used by others without the qualifications.

6. Research "facts" change over time, especially claims about human behavior. For example, all of the following research "facts" have been reported by major scientific sources, yet have been "refuted" by recent research evidence:

    Hostility and explosive anger heighten the risk of early death from heart disease and other illnesses.

    Left-handed people die at a younger age than right-handed people.

    Women under age 50 benefit from mammograms.

    A gene has been found that causes manic-depressive disorder.

7. Research varies in how artificial it is. Often, to achieve the goal of control, research loses some of its "real-world" quality. The more artificial the research, the more difficult it is to generalize from the research study to the world outside. The problem of research artificiality is especially evident in research studying complex social behavior. For example, to study the effects of television violence, researchers may expose children to vio-

lent cartoons and afterward observe how aggressive they are toward dolls. We should ask, "Is aggressive behavior toward dolls too artificial to tell us much about aggressive behavior in other situations?"

8. The need for financial gain, status, security, and other factors can affect research outcomes. Researchers are human beings, not computers. Thus, it is extremely difficult for them to be *totally* objective. For example, researchers getting directly funded by major drug companies may more frequently find positive treatment results for that company's drugs than researchers who have no personal relationship with the drug company. Also, pressures to get tenure and promotions, to maintain large grants, and to become famous may all influence the objectivity of the research findings.

As you can see, despite the many positive qualities of research evidence, we need to *avoid embracing research conclusions prematurely*. Being able to thoroughly and critically evaluate research requires an in-depth understanding of research methodologies and philosophies that this book cannot provide for you. We can, however, give you a number of questions that you can ask about research findings to help you decide whether they are dependable evidence:

1. What is the *quality of the source* of the report? Some sources of research tend to be more dependable than others. Usually, the most dependable reports are those that are published in peer-review journals, those in which a study is not accepted until it has been reviewed by a series of relevant experts. Usually—but not always—the more reputable the source, the better designed the study. So, try to find out all you can about the reputation of the source.

2. Other than the quality of the source, are there other clues included in the communication suggesting the research was well done? For example, does the report detail any *special strengths* of the research?

3. Has the study been *replicated?* Has more than one study reached the same conclusion? Findings, even when "statistically significant," can arise by chance alone. For example, when an association is repeatedly and consistently found in well-designed studies, like the link between smoking and cancer, then there is reason to believe it, at least until those who disagree can provide persuasive evidence for their point of view.

4. How *selective* has the communicator been in choosing studies? For example, have relevant studies with contradictory results been omitted? Has the researcher selected only those studies that support her point?

5. Is there any evidence of *strong-sense critical thinking?* Has the speaker or writer showed a critical attitude toward earlier research that was supportive of her point of view? Most conclusions from research need to be qualified because of research limitations. Has the communicator demonstrated a willingness to qualify?

6. Is there any reason for someone to have distorted the research? We need to be wary of situations in which the researchers *need* to find certain kinds of results.

7. Are conditions in the research *artificial* and therefore distorted? Always ask, "How similar are the conditions under which the research study was conducted to the situation the researcher is generalizing about?"

8. How far can we *generalize,* given the research sample? We discuss this question in depth in our next section.

9. Are there any *biases or distortions* in the surveys, questionnaires, ratings, or other measurements that the researcher uses? We need to have confidence that the researcher has measured accurately what she has wanted to measure. The problem of biased surveys and questionnaires is so pervasive in research that we discuss it in more detail in a later section.

Generalizing from the Research Sample

Speakers and writers usually use research reports to support generalizations, that is, claims about events in general. The ability to generalize from research findings depends on the *number, breadth,* and *randomness* of events or people the researchers study.

The process of selecting events or persons to study is called *sampling*.

Because researchers can never study all events or people about which they want to generalize, they must choose some way to sample; and some ways are preferable to others. You need to keep several important considerations in mind when evaluating the research sample:

1. The sample must be *large enough* to justify the generalization or conclusion. In most cases, the more events or people researchers observe, the more dependable their conclusion. If we want to form a general belief about how often college students receive help from others on term papers, we are better off studying 100 college students than studying 10.

2. The sample must possess as much *breadth,* or diversity, as the types of events about which conclusions are to be drawn. For example, if researchers want to generalize about college students' drinking habits *in general,* their evidence should be based on the sampling of a variety of different kinds of college students in a variety of different kinds of college settings. Students at a small private school in the Midwest may have different drinking habits than students at a large public school on the West Coast; thus, a study of students attending only one school would lack breadth of sampling.

3. The more *random* the sample, the better. When researchers randomly sample, they try to make sure that all events about which they want to generalize have an *equal chance* of getting sampled; they try to avoid a biased sample. Major polls, like the Gallop poll, for example, always try to

sample randomly. This keeps them from getting groups of events or people that have biased characteristics. Do you see how each of the following samples has biased characteristics?

a. People who volunteer to be interviewed about frequency of sexual activity.

b. People who are at home at 2:30 P.M. to answer their phone.

c. Readers of a popular women's magazine who clip and complete mail-in surveys.

Thus, we want to ask of all research studies, "How many events or people did they sample, how much breadth did the sample have, and how random was the sample?"

A common problem that stems from not paying enough attention to the limits of sampling is for communicators to *overgeneralize* research findings. They state a generalization that is much broader than that warranted by the research. Let's take a close look at an overgeneralization:

> Verbal abuse by professors is rampant on our campuses. A recent survey of 300 females at Brightsville College found that over 20 percent of them reported they had been verbally abused by at least one professor.

Sampling procedures prohibit such a broad generalization. The research report implies the conclusion can be applied to *all* campuses, when the research studied only one campus. We don't even know whether the conclusion can be applied to that campus, because we don't know how randomly researchers sampled from it. The research report is flawed because it greatly overgeneralizes.

Be alert to the possibility of speakers and writers overgeneralizing! It is a pervasive and powerful human disposition against which we must continually struggle.

Biased Surveys and Questionnaires

It's early evening. You have just finished dinner. The phone rings. "We're conducting a survey of public opinion. Will you answer a few questions?" If you answer "yes," you will be among thousands who annually take part in surveys—one of the research methods you will encounter most frequently. Think how often you hear the phrase "according to recent polls."

Surveys and questionnaires are usually used to measure people's attitudes and beliefs. Just how dependable are they? It depends! Survey responses are subject to many influences; thus, one has to be very cautious in interpreting their meaning. Let's examine some of these influences.

First, for survey responses to be meaningful, they must be answered *honestly*. That is, verbal reports need to mirror actual beliefs and attitudes. Yet, for a variety of reasons, people frequently shade the truth. For example, they may give answers they think they ought to give, rather than answers that reflect their true beliefs. They may experience hostility toward the questionnaire or toward the kind of question asked. They may give too little thought to the question. If you have ever been a survey participant, you can probably think of other influences.

Remember: *You cannot assume that verbal reports accurately reflect true attitudes.*

Second, many survey questions are ambiguous in their wording; the questions are subject to multiple interpretations. Different individuals may in essence be responding to different questions! For example, can you not imagine many interpretations of the following survey question: "Are you happily married?" The more ambiguous the wording of a survey, the less credibility you can place in the results.

You should always ask the question: "How were the survey questions worded?" Usually, the more specifically worded a question, the more likely that different individuals will interpret it similarly.

Third, surveys contain many *built-in biases* that make them even more suspect. Two of the most important are *biased wording* and *biased context*. Biased wording of a question is a common problem; a small change in how a question is asked can have a major effect on how a question is answered. Let's examine a conclusion based on a recent poll and then look at the survey question.

> A U.S. congressman sent a questionnaire to his constituents and received the following results: 92 percent were against government-supported child-care centers.

Now let's look closely at the survey question: "Do you believe the federal government should provide child-care centers to assist parents in rearing their children?" Look carefully at this question. Do you see the built-in bias? The "leading" words are "to assist parents in rearing their children." Wouldn't the responses have been quite different if the question had read: "Do you believe the federal government should provide child-care centers to assist parents who are unable to find alternative child care while they are working?" Thus, the responses obtained here are not an accurate indicator of attitudes concerning child-care centers.

Survey data and questionnaire must always be examined for possible bias. *Look carefully at the wording of the questions!* Here is another example. We have italicized the word that evidences the bias.

> QUESTION: Do you think that a person with a homosexual *disorder* should be permitted to teach your innocent children?

> CONCLUSION: Seventy-five percent of the people do not want homosexuals to teach their children.

The effect of *context* on an answer to a question can also be powerful. Even answers to identical questions can vary from poll to poll depending on how the questionnaire is presented and how the question is embedded in the survey. The following question was included in two recent surveys: "Do you think it should be possible for a pregnant woman to obtain a legal abortion if she is married and does not want any more children?" In one survey, the question was preceded by another question: "Should a woman be allowed to have an abortion if she had evidence that the fetus was defective?" In the other survey, no preceding question occurred. Not surprisingly, the two surveys showed different results. Can you see how the context might have affected respondents?

Another important contextual factor is *length*. In long surveys, people may respond differently to later items than to earlier items simply because they get tired. *Be alert to contextual factors when evaluating surveys.*

Because the way people respond to surveys is affected by many unknown factors, such as the need to please or the interpretation of the question, should we *ever* treat survey evidence as good evidence? There are heated debates about this issue, but our answer is "yes," as long as we are careful and do not overgeneralize further than is warranted. Some surveys are more reputable than others. The better the quality of the survey, the more you should be influenced by the results. Our recommendations is to examine survey *procedures* carefully before accepting survey *results*. Once you have ascertained the quality of the procedures, you can choose to generate your own *qualified generalization*—one that takes into account any biases you might have found. For example, if a survey has been completed using subscribers to a magazine associated with a liberal ideology then you would want to restrict any generalization found to people subscribing to that magazine. Even biased surveys can be informative; but you need to know the biases in order not to be unduly persuaded by the findings.

Critical Evaluation of a Research-Based Argument

Let's now use our questions about research to evaluate the following argument in which research evidence has been used to support a conclusion.

> Parents who try to keep their children from getting fat may wind up producing kids who don't know how to stop eating when they've had enough, a new study suggests. The study of 77 children ages 3 to 5 found that those with the most body fat had the most "controlling" mothers when it came to the amount of food eaten. "The more control the mother reported using over her child's eating, the less self-regulation the child displayed," Johnson and co-author Leann L. Birch said in the November issue of *Pediatrics*. The study was done at a preschool at the University of Illinois at Champaign-Urbana. The study found children whose mothers allowed them to be most spontaneous about food—eat when they are hungry and not necessarily finish all the food given to them—showed a natural instinct for regulating their own calories, the researchers said. "These internal cues, when interrupted, may well lead to overeating in later childhood, which could contribute to the child being overweight" said a pediatric nutritionist at Sanford University Medical Center.

In this communication, the research is presented in an uncritical fashion. We see no sign of strong-sense critical thinking. The communication uncritically accepts the findings. The original research study was published in a reputable journal, suggesting that it should be of high quality. The report makes no references to special strengths or weaknesses of the study, although it provides some detail of procedures so that we can make judgments about its worth as the basis of a generalization. There is no indication of whether the study has been replicated. Also, we do not know how selective the communicator has been in choosing studies, nor how this research fits into the broader context of research on causes of obesity. We do not know what benefits publishing this study may have had for the researchers, but we might speculate that publishing such research may help facilitate their getting grants or promotions, perhaps making them less cautious in making interpretations of their findings.

Have the researchers and passage author overgeneralized? The sample is fairly large—77—but it lacks breadth and randomness because it is restricted to one preschool in the Midwest. How were these children selected? How was the study advertised to the parents? Could there have been a bias in the kind of parents willing to sign up for such a study? Would we have gotten similar results if we had randomly chosen families from a large number of schools throughout the country? This passage clearly illustrates a case of overgeneralization!

Are the questionnaires biased? Contemplate being a parent and completing a questionnaire on how controlling you are? Don't you think we could raise doubts about the accuracy of responses to them? Too little information is given about the wording of the questionnaires or about the arrangement of questionnaire items to judge the ambiguity of the item wording and the possibility of biased wording and biased context.

We have raised enough questions about the above passage to be wary of the factual claims. We would want to rely on much more research before we could conclude that these claims are dependable.

Let's now look at a very different source of evidence.

Analogies As a Source of Evidence

Look closely at the structure of the following brief arguments, paying special attention to the reason supporting the conclusion.

> Education cannot prepare men and women for marriage. Trying to educate them for marriage is like trying to teach them to swim without allowing them to go into the water. It cannot be done.

> Who is responsible for all this unethical behavior in the present administration? It must be the president. After all, a fish rots from the head down.

> You wouldn't want to ingest a spoonful of arsenic into your system daily. I do not understand why you keep smoking. They both can kill you.

These three arguments use *analogies* as evidence, a very different kind of evidence from what we have previously been evaluating. How do we decide whether it is good evidence? Before reading on, try to determine the persuasiveness of the three arguments.

Communicators often attempt to prove a conclusion about something with which they are relatively *unfamiliar* by relying upon its similarity to something with which they are familiar. They use *resemblance* as a form of evidence. They reason in the following way: "If these two things are alike in one respect, then they will probably be alike in other respects as well."

For example, when researchers were first seeking the cause of AIDS, they identified diseases that seemed to share some similarities with AIDS, such as hepatitis, and tried to infer conclusions about the cause of AIDS on the basis of what they knew about the causes of these other diseases. We reason in a similar fashion when we choose to see a movie because a friend recommends it. We reason that because we resemble each other in a number of likes and dislikes, we will enjoy the same movie.

We will refer to an argument that uses a well-known similarity between two things as the basis for a conclusion about a relatively unknown characteristic of one of those things as an *argument by analogy*. Reasoning by analogy is a common way of presenting evidence to support a conclusion.

Analogies both stimulate insights and deceive us. For example, analogies have been highly productive in scientific and legal reasoning. When we infer conclusions about humans on the basis of research with mice, we reason by analogy. Much of our thinking about the structure of the atom is analogical reasoning. When we make a decision in a legal case, we base that decision on the similarity of that case to preceding cases; thus, we reason by analogy. Such reasoning can be quite persuasive.

Analogical reasoning can also be quite deceptive. The Ayatollah Khomeini, the former leader of Iran, for example, used an analogy to defend executing people convicted of adultery, prostitution, and homosexuality:

> If your finger suffers from gangrene, what do you do? You don't let the whole hand and then the body become filled with gangrene. No, you chop the finger off. So it is with corruption. We have to eliminate corruption.

Are gangrene and adultery, prostitution, and homosexuality *that* similar? Not at all. Thus, we have a very deceptive analogy. When certain societies burned people as though they were "witches," they acted on faulty analogical reasoning.

Because analogical reasoning is so common and has the potential to be both persuasive and faulty, you will find it very useful to recognize such reasoning and know how to systematically evaluate it. To evaluate the quality of an analogy, you need to focus on two factors.

1. The number of ways the two things being compared are *similar* and *different*.
2. The *relevance* of the similarities and the differences.

A word of caution! You can almost always find *some* similarities between any two things. So, analogical reasoning will not be persuasive simply because of many similarities. Strong analogies will be ones in which the two things we compare possess relevant similarities and lack relevant differences.

Let's check out the soundness of the following argument by analogy.

> I do not send my son outside when he is sick with flu or measles. Why should parents want to send their youngsters with AIDS to school? Are these children up to going to class? Do they feel like running, jumping, and playing when they are ill? You do not let your child go to school with the measles, so keep him at home if he has AIDS. After all, he is sick.

A major similarity between measles and AIDS that is potentially relevant to sending children to school is "having an illness." We note some relevant differences, however. Measles is associated with severe symptoms that gradually disappear, and the measles virus is easily transferred from one person to another. Development of symptoms from AIDS is very unpredictable, and there may be long periods without acute symptoms. It is not highly communicable because it is transferred through the blood. Thus, children with AIDS often feel well enough to want to attend school and, given our present state of knowledge, seem highly unlikely to pass the disease on to others. Because these differences should have some impact upon whether we keep a child out of school, they are relevant; thus, the analogy fails to provide strong support for the conclusion.

Another strategy that may help you evaluate reasoning by analogy is to *generate alternative analogies* for understanding the same phenomenon that the author or speaker is trying to understand. Such analogies may either support or contradict the conclusions inferred from the original analogy. If they contradict the conclusion, they then reveal problems in the initial reasoning by analogy.

For example, when authors argue that alcoholics should be eligible for health insurance, sick leave, and other benefits associated with inadvertent disease, they use a particular analogy to infer conclusions about alcoholics: alcoholism is like a biologically caused disease. Others, however, have generated an alternative analogy, arguing that alcoholism is like a "breakdown of the will." Note how thinking about this different analogy may create doubts about the persuasiveness of the original analogy.

A productive way to generate your own analogies is the following:

1. Identify some important features of what you are studying.
2. Try to identify other situations with which you are familiar that have some similar features. Give free rein to your imagination. Brainstorm. Try to imagine diverse situations.
3. Try to determine whether the familiar situation can provide you with some insights about the unfamiliar situation.

For example, in thinking about alcoholism, you could try to think of other situations in which people repeatedly seek immediate gratification despi potential long-term negative effects. Do smoking, eating, or gambling come to mind? Do they trigger other ways to think about alcoholism? You should now be capable of systematically evaluating the three brief analogical arguments at the beginning of this section. Ask the questions you need to ask to determine the structure of the argument. Then, ask the questions to evaluate the argument. Look for relevant similarities and differences. Usually, the greater the ratio of relevant similarities to relevant differences, the stronger the analogy. An analogy is especially compelling if you can find *no* relevant difference and you can find good evidence that the relevant similarities do indeed exist.

We found a relevant difference that weakens each of our three initial sample analogies. Check your evaluation against our list.

> (First example) The primary skills required for successful swimming are motor skills; many skills required for a successful marriage differ from motor skills. Such skills as money management and communication can be learned outside the context of marriage.

> (Second example) The "parts" of a political administration function much more independently than the parts of a fish. Unethical behavior at lower levels can result from complex and diverse causes.

> (Third example) In the case of arsenic, death is immediate and certain; in the case of smoking, death is statistically neither immediate nor certain. Also, smoking provides a great deal of immediate satisfaction; arsenic does not.

Summary

This chapter has continued our focus on the evaluation of evidence. We have discussed the following sources of evidence: observation, case studies, research studies, and analogies. Each source has its strengths and weaknesses. Usually, you can rely most on those claims that writers or speakers support directly by extensive scientific research. However, many issues have not been settled by scientific research, and consequently, communicators must rely on research that is not conclusive and on other sources of evidence. You should be especially wary of claims supported by biased observation, vivid case studies, poorly designed research, or faulty analogies. When you encounter *any* evidence, you should try to determine its quality by asking, *"How good is the evidence?"*

Practice Exercises

☞   *Critical Question:* **How good is the evidence?**

Evaluate each of these practice passages by examining the quality of the evidence provided.

Passage 1

The television show *Nightline* is symptomatic of what ails TV coverage in general. News and public affairs shows feature only a narrow spectrum of viewpoints, again and again. Real diversity is rare. For example, in 1989 the media watch group FAIR—Fairness & Accuracy in Reporting—issued the results of a tabulation of 40 months of *Nightline* shows—a total of 865 programs with 2,498 guests. The leading guests, with 14 appearances each, were Henry Kissinger and another former Secretary of State, Alexander Haig. Next came State Department official Elliott Abrams and the Moral Majority's Jerry Falwell (12 appearances each.) Out of the 19 American guests who could be termed *Nightline* "regulars" (more than five appearances), all were men, all but two were white, and 13 of the 19 were conservatives. "*Nightline*'s coverage of domestic and foreign affairs results in significant distortions," said the study. Essentially absent from the guest list are representatives of civic and community organizations, popular social movements, minority communities, and so on, the report found.

Passage 2

To what extent are adopted children more vulnerable to emotional and academic problems than their nonadopted peers? To answer this question, psychological and academic adjustments were evaluated in a sample of 130 adopted and 130 nonadopted children ranging in age from 6 through 11 years. Mothers and teachers rated the child's adjustment. Adoptive families were recruited from the New Jersey, Eastern Pennsylvania, and New York City areas through adoption support groups, adoptions agencies, newspaper advertisements, and word of mouth. Nonadoptive families were recruited from five central and northern New Jersey school systems and through newspaper advertisements. Adopted children were rated higher in psychological and school-related behavior problems and lower in social competence and school achievement than were nonadopted children. The results support the position that the risk of developing emotional and school-related problems is greater for adopted children.

Passage 3

We need a system of mandatory, consistent sentences for criminals. Let's assign numbers to each criminal act based upon its severity, then assign penalties accordingly. That is the only fair way to assure that we can get judges to dispense penalties in a just fashion. To assign a numerical value to a particular crime is not unlike equating a touchdown to six points or a field goal to three points.

Sample Responses

Passage 1

CONCLUSION: *News and public affairs shows fail to provide a diversity of viewpoints.*

REASON: *FAIR's study of* Nightline *found that male, white conservatives in positions of power dominated the guest list.*

The major evidence in this passage is a vivid case study. Thus, we must ask whether the case study is typical. The FAIR findings suggest the *possibility* that the news media *in general* presents the public with a narrow spectrum of views. Only *one* news show, however, was studied. We need to ask whether other news programs would show a similar pattern of guests before we judge the worth of the conclusion.

Passage 2

CONCLUSION: *The risk of developing emotional and school-related problems is greater for adopted children.*

REASON: *Adopted children are rated higher in psychological and school-related behavior problems and lower in social competence and school achievement than are non-adopted children.*

This is just a single study, and we would want to know how typical these results are of research in this area. We also cannot tell from the information given whether the study was published in a reputable journal. However, we can ask some useful questions about the study. The sample size is quite large, but its breadth is questionable. Although multiple states were sampled, to what extent were the family sizes, family incomes, and ages of parents typical of adoptive families? Perhaps the most important sampling problem was the lack of a random sample. Given the recruiting procedures, were there selective factors that led certain kinds of parents to volunteer for the study, and were these selective procedures different for adoptive and nonadoptive families? Perhaps, for example, adoptive families are generally more willing to volunteer even if their children are experiencing problems. If such selective factors were operating, then the sample is biased.

How accurate are the rating measurements? Can parent and teacher ratings be trusted to reflect emotional adjustment accurately? How objective are parents and teachers in making their ratings? Does knowing that the child is adopted affect how one rates that child? We would want to know more about the accuracy of these ratings before we could have much confidence in the conclusion.

Passage 3

CONCLUSION: *Fixed sentences for criminals are desirable.*

REASON: *Assigning sentences for a crime is like assigning points in a football game.*

The author is trying to demonstrate a relevant similarity: assigning points to a touchdown and assigning points to a crime. Also, a system of points makes a football game fair. But, assigning points to a criminal act is a much more complex process than assigning points to a touchdown. For example, whereas we do not see the circumstances of a football touchdown as relevant to how many points we give it, we might see the circumstances of a crime as highly relevant to how much punishment a criminal should receive. Also, we may desire flexibility and a human element in the very serious business of deciding on criminal penalties, something we would not desire in a football context—a game. It is possible that judges can better determine which penalty best fits the crime because of their experience and their familiarity with the case. Because of the many relevant differences, we conclude that this analogy is not very relevant.

Passage 4 (Self-Examination)

A recent study[1] shows evidence that modern boxers suffer brain damage from their sport. The researchers contacted by telephone 23 former boxers who (1) were aged 25 to 60 years, (2) were currently residing in the New York area, (3) had not retired from boxing for medical, neurological, or psychiatric reasons, (4) were retired from boxing for at least one year before the study, (5) had no known history of neurological, psychiatric, or serious medical illness, and (6) had no known history of drug or alcohol abuse. Eighteen former boxers volunteered to participate. The group included two former professional champions and three highly ranked professional contenders, and only one former fighter was primarily a "slugger"; all others were considered to be scientific, artful fighters who practiced self-defense.

Each boxer underwent neurological examinations, a computerized tomographic scan of the brain (a measure of brain atrophy), an electroencephalogram (EEG), and neuropsychological testing. The researchers found evidence of brain damage on at least two of the measures in 13 of the 15 professional boxers, and evidence of subtle brain damage in the three amateur boxers. The authors concluded that brain damage is a frequent result of a career in professional boxing.

[1]Adapted from I.R. Casson, O. Siegel, R. Shan, E.A. Campbell, M. Tarlau, and A. DiDomenico, "Brain Damage in Modern Boxers," *Journal of the American Medical Association* 251 (May 25, 1984), 2663–7.

10

Are There Rival Causes?

We begin this chapter with a story

> After carefully conditioning a flea to jump out of a box following the presentation of a loud noise, the researcher removed the first pair of legs to see what effect this had. Observing that the flea was still able to perform his task, the scientist removed the second pair of legs. Once again noting no difference in performance, the researcher removed the final pair of legs and found that the jumping behavior no longer occurred. Thus, the investigator wrote in his notebook, "When all the legs of a flea have been removed, it will no longer be able to hear."[1]

This story clearly illustrates a common goal in the use of evidence: answering the question, "What *caused* something to happen?" For example, what *caused*

[1]Adapted from Schuyler W. Huck and Howard M. Sandler, *Rival Hypotheses* (New York: Harper & Row, 1979), p. xiii.

the murder rate to decrease in the United States in 1996? Or, *why* has the rate of depression among teenagers increased over the last 10 years?

The story also shows a very common difficulty in using evidence to prove something caused something else—the problem of *rival causes*. The above fictional researcher offered one interpretation of his research findings: removal of the legs affected the flea's ability to hear. We expect that you can see that there is another very plausible interpretation of why the flea stopped jumping.

Thus, this story shows that the *same evidence* can be consistent with *different interpretations*. We refer to those different interpretations as rival causes. As we use the term, *rival cause* implies some alternative interpretation, different from the interpretation made by the communicator, for why events turned out as they did.

Although rival causes will rarely be as obvious as they are in our story, you will frequently encounter experts presenting one hypothesis to explain events or research findings when other plausible hypotheses could also explain them. Usually, these experts will not reveal rival causes to you; you will have to produce them. Doing so can be especially helpful as you decide "how good is the evidence?" because the existence of multiple, plausible rival causes for events reduces our confidence in the cause originally offered by the author.

Searching for rival causes will always be appropriate when a speaker or writer presents you with some evidence and offers a cause to explain it.

☞ *Critical Question:* **Are there rival causes?**

When to Look for Rival Causes

You need to look for rival causes when you have good reason to believe that the writer or speaker is using evidence to support a claim about the *cause* of something. The word *cause* means "to bring about, make happen, or affect." Communicators can indicate causal thinking to you in a number of ways. We have listed a few.

X has the effect of . . .	X deters . . .
X facilitates . . .	as a result of X . . .
X leads to . . .	X increases the likelihood . . .
X influences . . .	X determines . . .
X is a factor in . . .	X contributes to . . .
X is linked to . . .	

These clues to causal thinking should help you recognize when a communicator is making a causal claim. Once you note such a claim, be alert to the possibility of rival causes.

The Pervasiveness of Rival Causes

On Sunday evening, December 23, 1888, Vincent van Gogh, then 35 years old, cut off the lower half of his left ear and took it to a brothel, where he asked for a prostitute named Rachel and handed the ear to her, requesting that she "keep this object carefully."

Authors have offered numerous hypotheses to explain this event, including the following:

1. He was frustrated by two recent events: the engagement of his brother Theo, to whom he was very attached, and the failure of an attempt to establish a working and living relationship with Paul Gauguin. The aggressive impulses aroused by these frustrations were first directed at Gauguin, but then were turned against himself.[2]

2. Van Gogh had a great sympathy for prostitutes and identified with their status as social outcasts. One suggestion is that his self-mutilation was a reflection of this identification. "In June, just a few months before butchering his ear, he had written that 'the whore is like meat in a butcher shop' ; when he treated his own body as 'meat in a butcher's shop,' he reversed their roles, identified himself with the whore, and showed his sympathy for her."[3]

3. It is likely that Van Gogh experienced frightening auditory hallucinations during his psychotic attack similar to those he experienced in other attacks. Afterward, while in the sanitarium, he wrote that other patients heard strange sounds and voices as he had and speculated in one case that this was probably due to a disease of nerves in the ear. Thus, in a psychotic state, van Gogh could have felt that his own ear was diseased and cut it off to silence the disturbing sounds.[4]

Now, let's leave van Gogh's case for a moment and examine a different event in need of explanation—the findings of a research study.

A researcher reported that treating headaches with relaxation exercises and biofeedback is helpful. Three-fourths of 95 people with chronic tension headaches and about half of 75 migraine suffers studied reduced the frequency and severity of their headaches after learning how to relax head, neck, and shoulder muscles and control stress and tension with biofeedback.

In this study, the researcher probably began with the hypothesis that relaxation training causes reduction of headache suffering; and he found evidence consistent with that hypothesis. But let us offer several rival causes for the same findings.

---

[2]William M. Runyan, *Life Histories and Psychobiography* (New York: Oxford University Press, 1982), pp. 38–39.
[3]Ibid. p. 40.
[4]Ibid. pp. 40–41.

1. Research participants were highly suggestible, and the *expectation of improvement* was responsible for the change; like the sugar pill placebo effect in medicine, thinking they were going to get better might have stimulated a number of physical and mental processes that caused participants to feel better.

2. Participants wanted to please the researchers; thus, they reported feeling better even though they did not.

3. Most participants volunteered while undergoing highly stressful life situations; they experienced a reduction in life stress during the course of the study; and this reduction accounted for the reduction in symptoms.

Now, let's leave the research laboratory for a moment and move to the sports pages and examine some baseball statistics.

> During the 1996 season, the frequency of home runs hit in the major leagues showed a marked increase over the average number hit during the previous five years. Manufacturers of baseballs must be doing something to liven up the ball.

The hypothesis offered by the sportswriter is that a livelier baseball is causing the increase in home runs. But, let's again generate some rival causes:

1. Pitching quality markedly dropped during the 1996 season; there were many more injuries to pitchers than usual.

2. Weather patterns were unusual during the 1996 season; perhaps the air tended to be much less humid than usual. Reduced friction resulted in greater distance for each hit.

Now, let's examine some important lessons that can be learned from the van Gogh case, the research study, and the baseball statistics.

First, many kinds of events are open to rival causes, including clinical case studies, criminal trials, research studies, advertising statistics, sports page charts, airline crash findings, and historical events.

Second, experts can examine the same evidence and come up with different causes to explain it.

Third, although many explanations can "fit the facts," some seem more *plausible* than others.

Fourth, most communicators will provide you with only their favored causes—one that is subject to many biases; rival causes must be generated by the critical reader or listener.

Fifth, generating rival causes is a creative process; usually such causes will not be obvious. Thus, ability to generate causes varies.

Sixth, even "scientific" researchers frequently fail to acknowledge important alternative causes for their findings.

Finally, the worth of a particular cause is inversely related to the number of plausible rival causes.

(Incidentally, recent evidence suggests that van Gogh was actually suffering from an inner-ear infection) and that he cut off his ear to ease the excruciating pain.) In the following sections, we explore the implications of these lessons for the critical thinker.

Detecting Rival Causes

Locating rival causes is much like being a good detective. When you recognize situations in which rival causes are possible, you want to ask yourself questions like:

"Can I think of any other way to interpret the evidence?"

"What else might have caused this act or these findings?"

"If I looked at this from another point of view, what might I see as important causes?"

"If this interpretation is incorrect, what other interpretation might make sense?"

As you search for rival causes, try to *blind yourself to the author's interpretation* and see whether you can construct your own.

Rival Causes and Scientific Research

A major source of hypotheses about what causes events in our world is scientific research. Researchers start with tentative beliefs—hypotheses—about causes of events. For example, researchers generated many hypotheses about the cause of AIDS. One hypothesis was that AIDS is caused by a virus. Once a hypothesis has been firmly established by dependable research evidence, it changes from a hypothesis to a law. In the domain of complex human behavior, however, there are very few established laws. Beliefs like "TV violence cause crime," "passive smoke causes lung cancer," and "divorce causes juvenile delinquency" must currently all be viewed as hypotheses, not laws.

If that is the present state of affairs, what should you do when speakers or writers use findings from research studies to prove that one event causes another? Try to find out as much as you can about the research procedures used to produce the findings that support the hypothesis; then try to determine rival causes that might explain the findings. The more plausible rival causes that can account for the findings, the less faith we should have in the hypothesis favored by the communicator.

Because a major goal of scientific research is to minimize the number of plausible hypotheses for research findings, scientists have devised many techniques for ruling out, or eliminating, plausible rival causes. Sometimes these techniques work very well, and only a single hypothesis seems justifiably supported by the evidence. In such cases we can have some confidence in the dependability of that hypothesis. However, much research fails to rule out important rival causes, especially research that studies complex human behavior.

Let's use the following argument to practice detecting rival causes.

> Taking daily doses of vitamin E appears to cut the risk of heart disease between one-third and one-half, a major new study concludes. The results strengthen the newly popular belief that vitamins and other so-called antioxidants are good for the heart. Research findings were from the Nurses' Health Study, which enrolled 87,245 female nurses from across the United States. Seventeen percent of the nurses took vitamin E. During eight years of follow-up, 552 women suffered heart attacks. The researchers found that women who had taken vitamin E for more than two years had a 46 percent lower risk of a heart attack.

Should you rush out and buy vitamin E supplements? Not until you consider rival causes! How else might one explain these group differences?

First, let's outline the reasoning:

> CONCLUSION: *(Researchers' hypothesis)* Taking daily doses of vitamin E appears to cut the risk of heart disease between one-third and one-half.

> REASON: *(Researchers' evidence)* Research study showed women who had taken vitamin E had a lower risk of heart attack than those who had not.

Note that the words *appears to cut* in the conclusion tell us the researchers are making a causal claim about the evidence. But other hypotheses can explain this evidence.

The report fails to tell us why particular women took vitamin E. Isn't it possible that nurses who take vitamin E are the type of people who tend to maintain good health habits, such as exercising frequently and not eating fatty foods? If so, differences in exercise and eating habits are a plausible rival hypothesis that could explain the differences in heart attack risk between the two groups. Also, the women using vitamin E may be wealthier than the others and thus perhaps face a lower level of general life stress. We bet you can think of other reasons these two groups—vitamin E users and nonusers—differ in their risk of heart disease.

We cannot make you aware of all possible rival causes. In the following selections, however, we provide several clues for finding common rival causes.

Rival Causes for Differences between Groups

One of the most common ways for researchers to try to find a cause for some event is to *compare groups*. For example, you will frequently encounter the following kinds of references to group comparisons:

> Researchers compared an experimental group to a control group.
>
> One group received treatment X; the other group didn't.
>
> A group with clogged arteries was compared with a group without clogged arteries.

When researchers find differences between groups, they often conclude, "Those differences support our hypothesis." For example, a researcher might compare a group of cancer patients treated with a new drug with a control group of cancer patients that does not get the new drug, find that the groups differ in their recovery from cancer, and then conclude that the drug caused the difference. The problem is that *research groups almost always differ in more than one important way,* and thus group differences often are consistent with multiple causes. Thus, when you see communicators use findings of differences between groups to support one cause, always ask, "Are there rival causes that might also explain the differences in the groups?"

Let's take a look at a study that compares groups and try to detect rival causes.

> In a recent research study, Teacher A's teaching method for a psychology course was judged superior to that of Teacher B for that same course because Teacher A's class performed much better, on the average, than Teacher B's class on the same standardized, final, comprehensive multiple-choice test.

Here we have two groups: the classes of Teacher A and Teacher B. The question we need to ask is, "Did these two groups differ in important ways other than the teaching they experienced?" Did you think of either of the following possible important differences between the two groups that might account for test score differences?

Differences in average intelligence. It is possible that, on the average, more intelligent students signed up for Teacher A than for Teacher B, perhaps because they heard Teacher A was more challenging.

Differences in motivation. Perhaps one class was taught earlier in the day than another. Students who sign up for a class taught early in the day may be more motivated to learn than students who sign up for a class which is taught later in the day. Or perhaps the personalities of the two instructors differed greatly, influencing the motivation of the students.

You probably came up with other important differences. *Remember:* Many factors can cause research groups to differ!

Confusing Causation with Association

We have an inherent tendency to "see" events that are associated, or that "go together," as events that cause one another. That is, we conclude that because characteristic X (e.g., amount of TV viewing) is associated with characteristic Y (e.g., performance in school), that X therefore causes Y. The following are examples of such reasoning:

1. States with low speed limits tend to have a lower rate of highway death than states with higher speed limits; thus, low speed limits deter highway death.
2. Absence of a father in the home occurs at a higher rate with juvenile delinquents than with nondelinquents; thus, father absence is a cause of juvenile delinquency.

When we think this way, we are, however, often very wrong! Why? Usually, because multiple hypotheses can explain why X and Y "go together." In fact, there are at least four different kinds of hypotheses to account for any such relationship. Knowing what these are will help you discover rival causes. Let's illustrate each of the four with a research example.

A recent study reported that "hostility hurts women's health." The researchers studied 102 women over a 31-year period and found that women high in hostility at ages 21, 27, and 43 had more sickness at 52 than women low in hostility. "That includes everything from colds to serious illness." The researchers hypothesize that anger may release stress hormones or impair immunity.

Should women with a high degree of hostility be worried about their physical health? Not yet. Before they do, they should contemplate each of four potential explanations for the research findings.

Explanation 1: *X is a cause of Y.* (Hostility does indeed impair women's health.)

Explanation 2: *Y is a cause of X.* (Being in poor health may make women feel hostile.)

Explanation 3: *X and Y are associated because of some third factor, Z.* (Perhaps both hostility and poor health are caused by poor health-related behaviors, such as smoking and lack of exercise, or perhaps by stressful life events.)

Explanation 4: *X and Y influence each other.* (Perhaps feeling hostile weakens one's immune system, and in turn, a weaker immune system makes one feel tired, and this makes one feel more hostile.)

Remember: Association or correlation does not prove causation!

Yet much evidence to prove causation is only based on association or correlation. When an author supports a hypothesis by pointing to an association between characteristics, always ask, "Are there other causes that explain the association?"

Test yourself on the following:

A recent study reported that baldness is correlated with heart attack risk; bald-headed people have a higher risk of dying of an early heart attack than non-baldheaded people.

We hope you can now see that baldheaded people might be ill-advised to buy the newest hair-growing lotion to prevent a heart attack. What rival causes did you think of? Couldn't poor blood circulation or genetic inheritance account for the association between baldheadedness (X) and bad hearts (Y)?

Confusing "After this" with "Because of this"

Shortly after Clinton became president, the unemployment rate in the country dropped. Can we conclude that the Clinton presidency caused this drop? No. If we were to infer such a conclusion, we would be illustrating a very common way that people confuse causation with association.

Often, we try to explain a particular event as follows: Because event B *followed* event A, then event A *caused* event B. Such reasoning occurs because human beings have a strong tendency to believe that if two events occur close together in time, the first one must have caused the second one.

To appreciate the flaw in this reasoning, pick up today's newspaper and make a list of what is going on in the world. Then pick up yesterday's newspaper and make a similar list. Could you conclude that the events of yesterday are causing the events of today? Clearly not. For example, suppose yesterday's news reported that *Star Wars* broke all attendance records for movies and today's news reported that the stock market had dropped 20 points. It is highly unlikely that excitement about *Star Wars* caused the stock market to take a dip.

Many events that occur close together in time do not do so because one causes the other. When we wrongly conclude that the first event causes the second, we commit the *post hoc, ergo propter hoc* (meaning: "after this, therefore because of this") *fallacy*, or, for short, the *post hoc fallacy*. The following examples further illustrate the problem with this kind of reasoning.

> "Harry Hurricane must be an excellent coach; since he moved to our university, the team's record has improved dramatically." (But maybe the university also decided to double its athletic budget when Harry came.)

> "Since the Supreme Court decisions granting the accused more rights, the crime rate has steadily increased." (But maybe increases in unemployment have also occurred since those Supreme Court decisions.)

As you might guess, politicians are fond of using the *post hoc* argument, especially when it works in their favor. For example, they tend to take credit for anything good that takes place in the world after they come into office and to place blame elsewhere for anything bad that happens.

Remember: The finding that one event follows another in time does not by itself prove causation; it may be only a coincidence. When you see such reasoning, always ask yourself, "Are there rival causes that could account for the event?"

Caution: "After this, therefore because of this" reasoning may be, in certain instances, good reasoning. For example, if being invited to a dinner at the White House is consistently followed a week later by a major contribution by the dinner guest to the President's political party, then we should seriously consider the possibility that the dinner invitations may have a causal effect on political considerations.

DYNAMITE

Explaining Individual Events or Acts

Why did Bob Dole lose the 1996 election? What caused the downfall of the Dallas Cowboys in 1997? What caused the stock market to grow far beyond the experts' expectations in 1996? Why did Kurt Cobain die?

Like our question about van Gogh's ear, these questions seek explanations of individual historical events. Scientific research studies cannot answer the questions. Instead, we must search the past for clues. Such a search makes us highly susceptible to reasoning errors for several reasons. A couple of these are especially important to remember.

First, as we saw in the van Gogh case, so many different stories for the same event can "make sense." Second, the way we explain events is greatly influenced by social and political forces, as well as by individual psychological forces. For example, "liberals" might view the causes of homosexuality differently from "conservatives," and feminists might view the causes of anorexia much differently from physicians.

Also, a common bias is "the *fundamental attribution error*," in which we typically overestimate the importance of personal tendencies relative to situational factors in interpreting the behavior of others. That is, we tend to see the cause of other's behavior as coming from within (their personal characteristics) rather than from without (situational forces.) So, for example, when someone shows up late for a date, we're likely to view the lateness initially as a result of a tendency of the person to procrastinate or to be inconsiderate. However, we should also consider the role of unforeseen circumstances, such as car trouble, heavy traffic, or unanticipated company.

Another kind of common psychological error is to start with a limited number of possible causes and then to interpret additional information (even if it is irrelevant) as corroborating these existing hypotheses, rather than keeping the information separate or generating new, perhaps more complex, hypotheses. Our tendency is to simplify the world; yet often explanations require much complexity. Explaining events is not as simple as frequently portrayed by guest experts on the popular talk shows.

How can we know whether we have a "good" explanation of a particular event or set of events? We can never know for sure. But we can make some progress by asking critical questions. For example, we can ask:

Is there any evidence that the explanation has been critically examined?

Is it likely that the hypothesis may be *biased* by social, political, or psychological forces?

What *rival causes* have not been considered? How credible is the author's hypothesis relative to rival causes?

Is the hypothesis *thorough* in accounting for many puzzling aspects of the events in question?

How *consistent* is the hypothesis with all the valuable relevant evidence?

Be wary of accepting the first interpretation of an event you encounter. Search for rival causes and try to compare their credibility. Sometimes we must accept the fact that some events do not have a simple explanation.

Evaluating Rival Causes

The more plausible the rival causes that you come up with, the less faith you can have in the initial explanation offered, at least until further evidence has been considered. As a critical thinker, you will want to assess as best you can how each of the alternative explanations fits the available evidence, trying to be sensitive to your personal biases.

In comparing causes, we suggest that you apply the following criteria:

1. their logical soundness,
2. their consistency with other knowledge that you have, and
3. their previous success in explaining or predicting events.

Summary

Factual claims about the causes of events are weakened when other claims about the causes can be offered. Such claims are *rival causes.*

A common logical error in explaining observations is to confuse causation with association. Thus, always ask what other causes might explain observed associations. Be especially alert to the *post hoc fallacy.*

Practice Exercises

☞   *Critical Question:* **Are there rival causes?**

Each of the following examples provides an argument to support a causal claim.

Try to generate rival causes for such claims. Then try to determine how much you have weakened the author's claim by knowledge of rival causes.

Passage 1

A little bit of light may beat the winter blues. Researchers studied nine patients who suffered from winter depression, which is caused by the days getting shorter. The patients were exposed to bright fluorescent light upon awakening and in the late afternoon, for three hours at a time. Within a week, seven of the patients had recovered from their depression completely, and the other two showed a modest improvement. The light treatment works because it tricks the body into thinking that it's summer.

Passage 2

Why did the postal worker go berserk and kill those six employees? The answer is provided by a close look at his childhood. He lost his mother when he was 8, and his father often physically abused him. Also, he grew up in the shadow of more successful older siblings. As a child he had a difficult time making friends and had trouble establishing a sexual identity. Then, as an adult he drifted from job to job, while developing increasingly bizarre fantasies. Eventually, the post office became a symbol of the society that had caused his failures. To become "somebody," he ultimately turned to violence.

Passage 3

There are hopeful signs for American education today. For example, there are now real signs of progress in raising the learning level, at least among college-bound high school students. Scores of the 1985 Scholastic Aptitude Test (SAT) took the biggest upward leap in 21 years. For almost a decade scores have been gradually rising. After reaching an all-time low score in 1980 and 1981, the scores gained three points in 1982, stayed the same in 1983, increased a strong four points in 1984, and increased a whopping 9 points in 1985. Education Secretary William Bennett called the scores "further evidence that American secondary education is on the mend."[5]

Sample Responses

Passage 1

CONCLUSION: *Light treatment combats winter depression.*

REASONS: *Seven of nine patients exposed to light treatment completely recovered from their depression in a week's time.*

Can anything else account for the change besides light treatment? Yes; the researcher fails to rule out many obvious alternative explanations. For exam-

[5]Adapted from Dwight Bohmbach, *What's Right with America?* (New York: Bantam Books, 1986), p. 107.

ple, the patients might have *expected* to get better, and these *expectancies* might have led to feeling better. Also, they knew the purpose of the light treatment, and a rival cause is that they *tried to please* the researchers by reporting that they felt better. We can also hypothesize that external events during the one-week treatment period caused the change. Perhaps during the week of treatment, for example, the weather was especially good, and these people spent much more time exercising outside than usual. Another possibility is that these people were suffering from a form of depression from which they could naturally expect to recover in a short period of time. Can you locate other rival causes?

Passage 2

CONCLUSION: *The violent act of killing the post office workers was caused by experiencing a broken home, physical abuse, sibling rivalry, and loneliness in childhood.*

REASON: *The killer's childhood had these characteristics.*

It is possible that these childhood factors were important determinants of the acts of violence. But most people who have suffered such childhoods do not commit violent acts. Are there other possible causes for such behavior? As in the case of van Gogh, we suspect there may be many other plausible explanations. Before we could conclude that these childhood events were the causal factors, we would want to know more about this childhood and more about recent events in his life. For example, had he suffered any recent head injuries? Had he been using drugs? Had he had any recent highly stressful experiences with co-workers? After the fact, we can always find childhood experiences that make sense as causes of adult behavior. Before we draw causal conclusions, however, we must seek more evidence to prove that the one set of events caused the other than the mere fact that one set of events preceded the other set.

Passage 3

CONCLUSION: *Our education system is increasing the learning level, at least of college-bound high school students.*

REASONS: *SAT scores have shown a steady increase from 1981 to 1985.*

First, note that this essay attempts to explain a particular event—gradual increases in SAT scores by emphasizing one possible cause—an improvement in our educational system. Note also, that a *post hoc* reasoning logic is being used; SAT scores have increased following an effort to improve our educational system. Let's blind ourselves to the author's hypothesis and ask ourselves, "Can any other hypothesis explain the SAT score increases?"

One plausible explanation is that the nature of the population taking the test has been gradually shifting over time. For example, a larger number of less talented students may be choosing not to go to college, thus not taking the SAT; if so, the increases may reflect an increased proportion of higher-quality students taking the tests. Lots of other things were happening to these students in addition to their education during this five-year period. Has there been a gradual increase in attention to nutrition? Have parents increased their emphasis on education at home? Have students increased their motivation to achieve because of increasing concern about later job satisfaction? We expect that you can see that many rival causes can account for the facts presented in this essay.

Passage 4 (Self-Examination)

Diets that include meat are detrimental to the environment. To create food requires huge amounts of resources. Energy, water, and land are used for growing crops, feeding animals, and for food processing. The environment is damaged to the extent that these assets are used to create meat, rather than other things that we so desperately need.

A major cause of environmental degradation in this process is animal grazing. Thousands of trees are cut down annually to provide greater and greater amounts of grazing land. One result of the consequent reduction in the rain forest has been the extinction of 1,000 tropical species each year. Land is also destroyed as it is overgrazed.

Another negative consequence of meat consumption is water pollution. The resulting agricultural runoff includes manure and pesticides. The EPA has shown that runoff from farms is the largest source of pollution in our country. This polluting of our water leads to an increase in algae growth, which, in turn, kills other acquatic life.

11

Are the Statistics Deceptive?

How much should you be persuaded by the following passages?

> The National Coalition Against Domestic Violence estimates that more than half of married women (more than 27 million) will experience violence during their marriage, and that more than one-third (more than 18 million) are battered repeatedly every year.

> Women are better drivers than men, as proven by the fact that of men involved in accidents, 23 percent had been drinking—compared to 9.6% of the women.

You should not be very impressed by the above reasoning. Both arguments *deceive us with statistics!*

One of the most frequent kinds of evidence that authors present is "statistics." You have probably often heard people use the following phrase to help support their argument: "I have statistics to prove it." We use statistics (often inappropriately) to assess our nation's economic activity, to determine which TV shows will survive, to determine investment strategy, to help people decide on which sports teams to bet, to assess the country's social progress, to evaluate our sexual satisfaction, to predict the weather, and to provide input for many other issues.

Statistics are evidence expressed as numbers. Such evidence can seem quite impressive because numbers make evidence appear to be very scientific and precise, as though it represents "the facts." Statistics, however, can, and often do, lie! They do not prove what they appear to prove.

As a critical thinker, you should strive to detect erroneous statistical reasoning. In a few short chapters, we cannot show you all the different ways that people can "lie with statistics." However, this chapter will provide some general strategies that you can use to detect such deception. In addition, it will alert you to flaws in statistical reasoning by illustrating a number of the most common ways that authors misuse statistical evidence.

☞   *Critical Question: **Are the statistics deceptive?***

Unknowable and Biased Statistics

The first strategy for locating deceptive statistics is to try to find out as much as you can about how the statistics were obtained. Can we know precisely the number of people in the U.S. who have AIDS, have abortions, shoplift, commit white-collar crimes, engage in affairs, drink more than three beers a day, beat their wives, are homeless, or use cocaine? We suspect not. Why? Because there are a variety of obstacles to getting accurate statistics for certain purposes, including unwillingness to provide truthful information, failure to report events, and physical barriers to observing events. Consequently, statistics are often in the form of "educated guesses." Such estimates can be quite useful; they can also be quite deceiving. You will want to be sensitive to distorted estimates. Always ask, "How did the author arrive at the estimate?"

You can see the impact of this statistical deception in reports of wartime casualty figures. For example, America's defense intelligence agency estimated that 100,000 Iraqi soldiers died in the Persian Gulf War. But how were such figures obtained? We don't know the answer to that question, but we are wary of the preciseness of that figure because other sources have arrived at a casualty count of 8,000.

Another common place to find such errors is in reports of the incidence of various physical and medical disorders, especially when there is an effort to solicit attention to the disorder. For example, a recent book on eating disorders stated that every year 150,000 young women die of anorexia nervosa, and this number was frequently cited by the media. Others, alarmed by the frequency, took a closer look and found that 150,000 women *suffered* from eating disorders, but only 54 died in a recent year. These examples remind us to be wary of impressive or alarming numbers that are being used to persuade us.

Concluding One Thing, Proving Another

Communicators often deceive us when they use statistics that prove one thing to prove something different. The statistics don't prove what they seem to! We suggest two strategies for locating such deception.

One strategy is to *blind yourself to the communicator's statistics* and ask yourself, "What statistical evidence would be helpful in proving her conclusion?" Then, compare the needed statistics to the statistics given. If the two do not match, you may have located a statistical deception. The following example provides you with an opportunity to apply that strategy.

> A car dealer raved that a particular car was a big success because only 5 out of 100 buyers who bought the car had complained to the dealership about its performance. "When 95 percent of buyers are pleased," the salesman was heard to say, "then that's a darn good car."

How should the car dealer have proven his conclusion that 95 percent of buyers are pleased? Shouldn't he have randomly sampled a large number of buyers from among all buyers of that particular car and asked them, "Are you pleased with your car?" Instead, he has heard only from those who complained and assumed that all noncomplainers were pleased with the car, an unwarranted assumption. The dealer thus proves one thing (few buyers complained) and concludes another (most buyers were pleased). An important lesson to learn from this example is to *pay close attention to both the wording of the statistics and the wording of the conclusion* to see whether they are referring to the same thing. If they are not, the author or speaker may be lying with statistics.

It is frequently difficult to know just what statistical evidence should be provided to back up a conclusion. Thus, let us suggest a further strategy. Examine the author's statistics *very closely* while *blinding yourself to the conclusion;* then ask yourself, "What is the appropriate conclusion to be drawn from those statistics?" Then, compare your conclusion with the author's. Try that strategy with the following example.

> Almost one-fourth of psychotherapists have sexually abused patients who were minors. A clinical psychologist surveyed distinguished psychologists around the country. Of the 90 who replied to the survey, 24 percent said they knew of instances in which therapists abused minor patients.

Did you come up with the following conclusion? Almost one-fourth of therapists *know about* instances when therapists abused minor patients. Do you see the difference between what the statistics proved and what the author concluded? If so, you have discovered how this author has lied with statistics.

Now, practice on the following.

> In 1985, a newspaper columnist asked female readers, "Would you be content to be held close and treated tenderly and forget about 'the act'?" She reported that

72 percent of the respondents answered "yes" and concluded, "The survey means that a tremendous number of women out there are not enjoying sex."

Do you see how the writer has concluded one thing while proving another? Do you think results might have been different if the columnist had asked, "Are you enjoying sexual activity?"

Deceiving by Omitting Information

Statistics often deceive us because they are incomplete. Thus, a further helpful strategy for locating flaws in statistical reasoning is to ask, *"What further information do you need before you can judge the impact of the statistics?"* Let's look at two examples to illustrate the usefulness of this question.

1. A crime wave has hit our city. Homicides have increased by 67 percent in the last year.
2. Boxing is less dangerous than other contact sports. A survey of sports-related deaths in New York City over a 30-year period revealed that baseball, with 43 deaths, led both football (22) and boxing (21) in terms of mortality.

At first, 67 percent seems quite impressive. But something is missing: the absolute numbers on which this percentage is based. Wouldn't we be less alarmed if we knew that this increase was from three homicides to five, rather than from 300 to 500? In our second example, we have the numbers, but we don't have the percentages. Wouldn't we need to know what these numbers mean in terms of percentages of athletes involved in the sports? After all, there are fewer total boxers than there are baseball players.

When you encounter impressive-sounding numbers or percentages, be wary. You may need to get other information to decide just how impressive the numbers are.

Another important kind of potential missing information is *relevant comparisons*. It is often useful to ask the question, "As compared to . . .?"

Each of the following statements illustrates statistics that can benefit from asking for comparisons:

1. Fizz aspirin works 50 percent faster.
2. Funding for AIDS research is more than adequate. Last year the government spent over $1.2 billion on AIDS research.
3. College degrees pay off. A recent survey found that workers with a bachelor's degree were earning an average of $31,500 per year in the spring of 1996.

With reference to the first statement, don't you need to ask, "Fifty percent faster than what?" Other ineffective aspirins? Previous Fizz aspirin? As for the second statement, wouldn't you want to ask how the expenditure compares to previous years, or to research on other diseases, or to the total spent by the government on health-related research? With reference to the third statement, how does that average compare to the average earnings of equally intelligent people who decided not to go to college?

When you encounter statistics, be sure to ask, "What relevant information is missing?"

Summary

We have highlighted a number of ways by which you can catch people "lying" with statistics. We hope that you can now see the problems with statistics on domestic violence and on driving ability that we presented at the beginning of the chapter. *Hints:* Where did that impressive figure of more than 27 million come from? If you were to use statistics to compare male and female driving ability, wouldn't you be primarily interested in the number of accidents per mile driven, rather than in the statistics provided?

The following is a summary of ways you can detect deceptive statistics:

1. Try to find out as much as you can about how the statistics were obtained. Ask, "How does the author or speaker know?"
2. Be alert to users of statistics concluding one thing, but proving another.
3. Blind yourselves to the writer's or speaker's statistics and compare the needed statistical evidence with the statistics actually provided.
4. Form your own conclusion from the statistics. If it doesn't match the author's or speaker's, then something is probably wrong.
5. Determine what information is missing. Be especially alert for misleading numbers and percentages and for missing comparisons.

Practice Exercises

☞   *Critical Question:* **Are the statistics deceptive?**

For each of the four practice passages, identify inadequacies in the evidence.

Passage 1

Americans in general are spoiled. Most of us tend to judge the times in relative terms—and we have had rich relatives.

Materially, no people on earth have ever been as well off. So, when most of us say "times are bad," we say it in a comfortable home, with a well-stocked electric refrigerator, television, and electric laundry equipment.

One in every five households in America in 1980 was affluent (had an income over $25,000). Twenty-five years ago, only 1 in 33 households was this comfortable. Our personal income, disposable income, and personal savings have all climbed continuously since 1950.

True, we still have a vast army of poor in the country. One in every eight Americans is living below the poverty level—one in every four aged 65 or over is poor. But 20 years ago, one in every five citizens was below the poverty line. In seven years, more than 14 million of us have climbed out of the poverty hole.

Any country in which, while population increased 56 percent, homeownership increased 100 percent, car ownership 130 percent, and personal savings 696 percent, is a long way from hard times. All that happened here between 1946 and 1980!

Passage 2

"It just isn't safe to drive anymore," my friend lamented, shaking his head as we tooled through Friday afternoon traffic on the freeway. But the fact is, driving in America is safer than it's been in over 60 years. In 1984, we had 18.4 traffic fatalities per 100,000 population, compared to 25.8 in 1970 and 23.3 in 1950. Today you're a lot safer on the road in your car than you are at home or at work. Twelve out of 100 Americans are laid up or need medical attention during the year because of household accidents. Five out of 100 get hurt at work. But only 2.2 per 100 are injured in automobile accidents.[1]

Passage 3

Vehicle theft is on the rise on our campuses. A recent study by Dr. Adam Johnson found that 83 percent of the 100 colleges and universities that he studied have experienced an increase in vehicle theft between 1994–1996. More than half of these schools experienced a greater than 20 percent jump in the three-year period.

Trying to go into even greater depth, Professor Johnson in 1997 asked students on the same 100 campuses whether they were more concerned about crime now than they were in 1994. They overwhelmingly responded that crime was more on their minds now.

Our campuses are experiencing a new crime wave.

Sample Responses

Passage 1

CONCLUSION: *Materially, times are not bad.*

REASONS: *1. More households are affluent today. One in every five households in 1980*

[1]Michael Bohmbach, *What's Right with America* (New York: Bantam, 1986), p. 36.

was affluent, with over $25,000 in income. Twenty-five years ago, only 1 in 33 was comfortable.

2. *Our personal income, disposable income, and personal savings have all climbed since 1950.*

    a. *Fewer Americans—one in every eight rather than one in every five—are below the poverty level. In seven years, more than 14 million of us have climbed out of poverty.*

    b. *While population has increased 56 percent, home ownership has increased 100 percent, car ownership 130 percent, and personal savings 696 percent between 1946 and 1980.*

First, let's look at the first reason. The writer compares ratios—one in five versus 1 in 33. Is this comparison legitimate? No. A very important piece of information has been omitted. What income was needed to be affluent 20 years ago? He has failed to take inflation into account. Using this same logic, probably only 1 in 1,000 would have been comfortable 50 years ago.

The first part of the evidence for the second reason suffers from the same problem. This evidence cannot be judged until we know how "poverty level" is defined. If the definition has not taken inflation into account or has changed in its basic meaning over time, then these ratios cannot be legitimately compared. Also, in Reason 2a, the writer has tossed out an impressively large number—14 million. What percentage does that reflect? Has he taken population growth into account?

Reason 2b presents impressive percentage differences, but what do those percentages mean? Percentages of what? For example, is the homeownership figure based on the percentage of people who own homes, or on the absolute number of homes owned? To judge these percentages, we need to know how they were figured and the absolute numbers on which they were based.

While population has increased 56 percent, what has been the increase in numbers of families or potential home buyers?

Without the omitted information, the evidence presented does not adequately support the conclusion.

Passage 2

CONCLUSION: *Driving in America is much safer now than it was 60 years ago.*

REASONS: 1. *Traffic fatalities have decreased greatly from 1950 to 1984.*

            2. *It's now safer to drive than it is to stay at home. Data reveal that you are less likely to have an accident in your car than you are at home or at work.*

To evaluate this use of evidence, we should first ask ourselves what would be the most appropriate evidence to address the question, "Is driving in America safer than it used to be?" In our opinion, the best statistic to use to answer that question is a comparison of the rate of serious accidents per specified numbers of miles driven under certain kinds of conditions—for example, city and highway driving—between the present and the past. Those are not the figures given in the essay. The figures given are rates per *100,000 population;* thus the comparison is deceiving. For example, is the per capita mileage driven in 1984 the same as that driven in 1950 and 1970?

The second set of evidence also represents a deceptive comparison because the figures given fail to take into account the fact that we spend much more time in our offices and in our homes than we do in our cars. The appropriate statistic to be used here would be the rate of accidents per hour spent in each setting; note how that rate differs radically from the percentages actually given. (*Note:* The argument presented here is similar to arguing that it's safer for a woman to walk in New York's Central Park than to read in her home, because a larger percentage of rapes occur in the home than in parks.)

Passage 3

CONCLUSION: *Campus crime is on the rise.*

REASONS: 1. *A study found that vehicle theft is increasing on a large number of campuses.*
2. *Students feel more concern about crime now than they did before the study was conducted.*

The first part of this argument compiles evidence leading to one conclusion, but the passage concludes something else. If the study is valid, it proves that vehicle theft is on the rise in the three-year period of the study. But it does not provide adequate support for the conclusion that campus crime is on the rise. Campus crime comes in many forms, in addition to vehicle theft. For all we know from the study, bike thefts may be up, while assaults, murder, and rape have dropped to all-time lows on college campuses.

In addition, we would want to know more about the sample for the study. Is the sample of campuses broad and large enough to provide a fair representation of typical college life? Did the definition of vehicle theft stay the same during the three-year period? Do all the campuses use the same definition of "vehicle theft" when they gather the reported statistics? These are just a few of the questions that we would want the professor to answer before we placed much confidence in his study. The second reason is not very persuasive either unless we know more information about the statistic. Did the student respondents know, for example, that Dr. Johnson was a well-known critic of unsafe campuses and, thus, probably wanted them to be fearful of campus crime? Which students were asked on the sampled campuses? Do these students have any special reason to perceive or report a crime wave? Finally, just how much more concerned are the respondents and how are they measuring their concern? It is quite possible that the students who are more concerned about crime are just a trace more concerned, while those who perceive a reduced threat of crime are intensely convinced that crime is a much more minor problem now.

Passage 4 (Self-Examination)

The cafeteria food on our campus is worse than it has ever been. Nine out of 10 students tell us that they prefer to eat off campus at least once a day because they can't stand the food. Only 5 percent of students agreed in a survey with the statement that "I like the majority of the cafeteria food that I eat." Off-campus restaurants regularly advertise that "our food is hard to beat." Finally, a local lasagna company that was trying to confirm the high quality of its pasta was shocked to find that only one student stopped at its booth outside the cafeteria to compliment the company on its lasagna.

12

What Significant Information Is Omitted?

How compelling are the following advertisements?

Most doctors prescribe Ease-Pain for headaches!

Coke was Number 1 in recent taste tests!

The purpose of both advertisements is, of course, to persuade you to buy more of the designated product. Even before your critical-thinking skills developed to their current level, you knew that such advertisements tell less than the whole truth. For example, if the Ease-Pain company gives bigger discounts to hospitals than other aspirin manufacturers, provides hospitals with greater numbers of free samples, or provides cruises for physicians who use their product, you are unlikely to see this information included in the ad—even though it may be highly relevant to judging the merit of the advertising claim.

By asking questions learned in previous chapters, such as those concerning ambiguity, assumptions, and evidence, you will detect much important missing information. A more complete search for omitted information, however, is so important to critical evaluation that it deserves further emphasis. This chapter tries to sensitize you even more to the importance of *what is not said* and to serve as an important reminder that we react to an incomplete picture of an argument when we evaluate only the *explicit* parts. We thus devote this chapter to an extremely important additional question you must ask in order to judge the quality of reasoning: What significant information is omitted?

☞   *Critical Question:* **What significant information is omitted?**

The Benefits of Detecting Omitted Information

You should remember that information that you encounter has a purpose. In other words, its organization was selected and organized by someone who hoped that it would affect your thinking in some way. Hence, your task is to decide whether you wish to be an instrument of the chosen purpose. Often that purpose is to persuade you.

Advertisers, teachers, politicians, authors, speakers, and parents all organize information to shape your decisions. It is a natural and highly predictable desire on their part. Thus, those trying to persuade you will almost always try to present their position in the strongest possible light. So when you find what you believe to be persuasive reasons—those gold nuggets for which you are prospecting—it's wise to hesitate and to think about what the author may *not* have told you, something that your critical questioning has not yet revealed. These reasons may not be quite so impressive if you realize that their apparent support for the conclusion rests on significant information that has been omitted.

By *significant omitted information,* we mean information that would affect whether you should be influenced by a speaker's or writer's arguments, that is, information that *shapes the reasoning!* Interspersed throughout the chapter will be examples of reasoning that is not very convincing, not because of what is said but because of what is omitted. Study the examples carefully and notice how in each case the failure to look for omitted information would have resulted in your making a premature judgment.

The Certainty of Incomplete Reasoning

Incomplete reasoning is inevitable for several reasons. First, there is the limitation imposed by time and space. Arguments are incomplete because communicators do not have forever to organize them, nor do they have unlimited space or time in which to present their reasons.

Second, most of us have a very limited attention span; we get bored when messages are too long. Thus, communicators often feel a need to get their message across quickly. Advertisements and editorials reflect both these factors. For example, the time or space allotted for presenting an advertising message is short, and the message must both attract and hold our attention. Advertisers consequently engage in many annoying omissions.

A third reason for the inevitability of missing information is that the knowledge possessed by the person making the argument will always be incomplete. For example, no one can know everything about the former relationship between Nicole Brown and O.J. Simpson. Consequently anyone claiming to know how Mr. Simpson was feeling on the night that Nicole was killed must be omitting information that would be helpful to you if you were carefully trying to make up your mind about the state of his mind on that night. Similarly, when over half the doctors sampled in a survey of attitudes toward national health insurance fail to complete the questionnaire, it is impossible to know whether they differ in significant ways from the doctors who do complete the survey. Yet this is a very important piece of information.

A fourth reason why information may be omitted is because of an outright attempt to deceive. Advertisers *know* they are omitting key bits of information. If they were to describe all the chemicals or cheap component parts that go into their products, you would be less likely to buy them. Experts in every field consciously omit information when open disclosure would weaken the persuasive effect of their advice. Such omissions are particularly tempting if those trying to advise you see you as a "sponge."

A final important reason why omitted information is so prevalent is that the values, beliefs, and attitudes of those trying to advise or persuade you are frequently different from yours. You can expect, therefore, that their reasoning will be guided by different assumptions from those you would have brought to the same question. A particular perspective is like a pair of blinders on a horse. The blinders improve the tendency of the horse to focus on what is directly in front of it. Yet, an individual's perspective, like blinders on a horse, prevents that person from noting certain information that would be important to those who reason from a different frame of reference. Unless your perspective is identical to that of the person trying to persuade you, important omissions of information are to be expected.

Let's review. Omitted information is inevitable. There are at least five reasons for the prevalence of omitted information:

1. time and space limitations
2. limited attention span
3. inadequacies in human knowledge
4. deception
5. different perspectives

Do you now see the danger of the sponge model even more clearly? You must actively question expertise and advice if you are to avoid forming opinions based on unnecessarily limited information.

Questions That Identify Omitted Information

If you are now convinced that reasoning will necessarily be incomplete, you may ask, "What am I supposed to do?" Well, initially you have to remind yourself again and again that regardless of how attractive the reasons supporting a particular decision or opinion may be at first glance, it's necessary to take another look in search of omitted information. How do you search, and what can you expect to find? You ask questions to help decide what additional information you need, and then ask questions designed to reveal that information.

Isn't it silly to ask questions of an author who cannot answer? Not at all! Although the writer won't answer your questions, asking her has positive results. First, you may be able to supply the missing information because of what you already know. Second, searching for omitted information in persuasive writing gives you good practice for when you are able to search for omitted information face-to-face with a teacher or anyone else who is trying to persuade you orally. Even more importantly, searching for missing information prevents you from making up your mind too soon. By asking such questions of written material, you are reminding yourself that the information provided is incomplete and that whatever conclusion you reach on the basis of incomplete information will necessarily be very tentative. You cannot feel very confident about your opinion as long as important information is missing.

There are many different kinds of questions you can use to identify relevant omitted information. Some questions you have already learned to ask will highlight important omitted information. For example, asking critical questions about ambiguity, the use of evidence, and the quality of assumptions usually identifies relevant omitted information.

In addition, to help you determine omitted information that might get overlooked by other critical questions, we provide you below with a list of some important kinds of omitted information and some examples of questions to help detect them. Being aware of these specific types should help you a lot in locating relevant omitted information. Because there are so many kinds of important omitted information, however, you should always ask yourself the general question, "Has the speaker or writer left out any other information that I need to know before I judge the quality of her reasoning?"

Here are common kinds of significant omitted information:

1. **Common counterarguments**
   a. What reasons would someone who disagrees offer?
   b. Are there research studies that contradict the studies presented?
   c. Are there missing examples, testimonials, or analogies that support the other side of the argument?
2. **Missing definitions**
   a. How would the arguments differ if key terms were defined in other ways?

3. **Missing value preferences or perspectives**
   a. From what other set of values might one approach this issue?
   b. What kinds of arguments would be made by someone approaching the issue from a different set of values?
4. **Origins of "facts" alluded to in the argument**
   a. Where do the "facts" come from?
   b. Are the factual claims supported by well-done research or by reliable sources?
5. **Details of procedures used for gathering facts**
   a. How many people completed the questionnaire?
   b. How were the survey questions worded?
6. **Alternative techniques for gathering or organizing the evidence**
   a. How might the results from an interview study differ from written questionnaire results?
7. **Missing or incomplete figures, graphs, tables, or data**
   a. Would the figure look different if it included evidence from earlier or later years?
   b. Has the author "stretched" the figure to make the differences look larger?
8. **Omitted effects, both positive and negative, and both short- and long-term, of what is advocated and what is opposed**
   a. Has the argument left out important positive or negative consequences of a proposed action?
   b. Do we need to know the impact of the action on any of the following areas: political, social, economic, biological, spiritual, health, or environmental?
9. **Context of quotes and testimonials**
   a. Has a quote or testimonial been taken out of context?
10. **Benefits accruing to the author from convincing others to follow her advice**
    a. Will the author benefit financially if we adopt her proposed policy?

Let's examine some arguments that have omitted some of the types of information listed above and watch how each omission might cause us to form a faulty conclusion. Only by asking that omitted information be supplied in each case could you avoid this danger. Initially, let's look at an advertising claim.

A well-known mouthwash commercial boasts that the mouthwash has new powerful ingredients that kill 90 percent of the bacteria that cause bad breath. Should we thus conclude that we should buy this advertised brand of mouthwash? Wait just a minute! Among many omissions, the advertisement neglects to include any information about: (a) what percentage of bacteria other mouthwashes kill; maybe they kill 95 percent of the bacteria; (b) amount of bacteria killed by regular brushing of teeth or by simply swishing water around in our mouth; maybe our breath is fine as long as we brush our teeth; (c) potential negative consequences of killing mouth bacteria; maybe a certain amount of bacteria is necessary for a healthy mouth; (d) other causes of bad breath; maybe tonsils and sinus infections contribute; (e) how much bacteria are needed to cause bad breath; maybe 10 percent is enough; (f) the effect of the mouthwash on the inside of the mouth; might it harm our gums? (g) other advantages and disadvantages of the mouthwash, such as taste, price, and length of effective action. The advertiser has omitted much significant data that you would need if you were to buy wisely.

Do you see how advertising phrases like "doctor recommended," "it's the real thing," "reduced calories," "light," "98 percent fat free," "fiber rich," "can help to reduce cholesterol," and "100 percent natural," may all be accurate but misleading because of omitted information?

It's pretty obvious that advertising omits much relevant information. Let's now take a look at a more complicated reasoning example. Read the following excerpt and ask yourself what has been omitted, referring to our list for clues to your search.

> Women in our society are paying a steep price for feminism's push for increased equality. By delaying marriage to pursue careers, women encounter a severe "man shortage," endangering their opportunity for marriage. For example, a recent marriage study by Harvard and Yale researchers found that a college-educated, unwed woman at 30 has a 20 percent likelihood of marriage, and at 35, a 5 percent chance. In addition, there has been a major plunge in economic status afflicting women who divorce under the new no-fault law. A study by a sociologist found that the average woman suffers a 73 percent drop in her living standard a year after divorce, while the average man enjoys a 40 percent rise. Also, women's mental health has never been worse and is declining in direct proportion to women's tendency to stay single or devote themselves to careers. In fact, single women now make up the great majority of psychotherapists' practice.

What important information do you need to know before you can decide whether feminists should stop pushing for equality with men? Let us suggest some questions.

What common counterarguments or counterexamples might feminists use to refute this reasoning? We can imagine counterarguments that stress the positive consequences of seeking greater equality, such as increased diversity in job choices and domestic roles, increased legal rights, and increased reproductive freedom.

What are possible definitions of mental health that might be used in this argument? What value assumptions do these definitions reflect?

What is the origin of the facts alluded to in the argument? How does the author know that women's mental health has declined and that single women dominate psychotherapists' offices and that the average woman suffers a 73 percent drop in her living standard? Also, how confident can we be of the calculation of marital odds? The research appears to originate from university settings, but the author presents too little detail for us to judge the quality of the research.

For example, is it helpful to you to know that in a more recent study than the one cited, another university researcher sampled 13.4 million households, instead of the 60,000 sampled in the cited study, and found that at 30, never-married, college-educated women have a 58 to 66 percent chance at marriage, and at 35 the odds were 32 to 41 percent, seven times higher than the Harvard–Yale figure? We would surely want to know the basis for this difference before we judge the quality of the evidence cited.

Would other research methods give us a different view of women's happiness? For example, we can tell you that a 1990 study, which tracked the same women for more than three decades, reported that "traditional" married women ran a higher risk of developing mental and physical ailments in their lifetime than single women—from depression to migraines, from high blood pressure to colitis. Also, a 1989 Louis Harris poll of women between 45 and 60 reported that the majority of them said they didn't want to get married.

How do the living standards of divorced women and men differ after *five* years? Obviously, the author gave you only a partial picture of how feminist goals of equality have affected women. Unless you complete the picture, your decision about whether to support feminist goals will be very uninformed.

The Importance of the Negative View

There is one type of omitted information that we believe is so important to identify and so often overlooked that we want to specifically highlight it for you: *the potential negative effects* of advocated actions, such as new technology, industrial expansion, and public policy. We stress the negative effects here because usually proposals for such action come into existence in the context of backers heralding their benefits, such as greater choice and speed, better appearance, more leisure, increased length of life, and more and/or improved commodities. However, because most actions have such widespread positive *and negative* impacts, we need to ask:

- Which segments of society do *not* benefit from a proposed action? Who loses? What do the losers have to say about it?
- How does the proposed action affect the distribution of power?
- Does the action influence the extent of democracy in our society?
- How does a particular action affect how we view the world: what we think, how we think, and what we know and can know?
- What are the action's effects on our health?

For each of these questions, we always also want to ask, "What are the potential *long-term negative effects* of the action?"

To illustrate the usefulness of asking these omitted-information questions, let's reflect upon the following question: What are some possible negative effects of increasing advances in computer technology, a policy advocated by many in our society? Did you think of the following?

- *Pollution and impaired health.* For example, does computer manufacturing use large amounts of toxic materials that must eventually be disposed of at toxic dumps? Also, what is the effect on our health of lengthy periods in front of a computer terminal?
- *Shifts in employment.* How many people might lose their jobs or have to shift to less interesting jobs?
- *Invasion of privacy.* How easy will it be for others to possess information about our incomes and our personal habits?
- *Information acceleration.* What is the effect on human beings of an information overload?
- *Military centralization.* Is it possible that with increased connections among super computers, individual groups in our society might gain too much power over military actions?

Questions such as these can give us pause for thought before jumping on the bandwagon of a proposed action.

Omitted Information That Remains Missing

Just because you are able to request important missing information, does not guarantee a satisfactory response. It is quite possible that your probing questions cannot be answered. Do not despair! You did your part. You requested information that you needed to make up your mind; you must now decide whether it is possible to arrive at a conclusion without the missing information. We warned you earlier that reasoning is always incomplete. Therefore, to claim automatically that you cannot make a decision as long as information is missing would prevent you from ever forming any opinions. The information you need to be perfectly certain that you are right will never be available.

Practice Exercises

☞   *Critical Question:* ***What significant information is omitted?***

In each of the following examples, there is important missing information. Make a list of questions you would ask the person who wrote each passage. Explain in each case why the information you are seeking is important to you as you try to decide the worth of the reasoning.

Passage 1

Students need more sleep. Their performance on papers and exams deteriorates as they get less sleep. Again and again, when honors students are asked about their sleep habits, they tell us that they get a lot of sleep.

Further, we have all seen the late-night parade of students coming home late from the bars. Our counseling center published a pamphlet that documented the fact that these late-night carousers are often the very students who are eventually dismissed from campus because of poor grades. A little more sleep might have rescued them.

Passage 2

Doctors and medical experts across the nation need to keep up the effort of urging Americans to reduce their intake of cholesterol and saturated fats. A diet high in cholesterol and saturated fats has been linked to a high incidence of coronary disease. A survey comparing the food intakes of 1,500 women in 1977 and a similar group in 1985 demonstrates that the warnings of health experts have not been in vain. The findings of the survey reveal that women are consuming 35 percent less whole milk, 34 percent less red meat, and 28 percent fewer eggs. The findings also indicated a 60 percent increase in skim milk consumption and a 29 percent increase in whole grain consumption. Better decisions in the supermarket are resulting in dramatic improvements in the health of American women.

Passage 3

Researchers long have sought a "morning-after" pill that could make birth control safer and effective than it is today. A study in Scotland suggests that such a pill soon may be available. But abortion opponents are trying to block its use in the U.S. The study tested small doses of RU-486, the controversial French abortion drug, on 402 women, and no pregnancies resulted. The drug caused fewer side effects than the less-than-satisfactory morning-after pills available from doctors today. If tested and eventually sold here, RU-486 might save women from undergoing abortions and from running gauntlets of screaming, sign-waving protesters. RU-486 is relatively safe, simple, and cheap. We need to stop the abortion opponents from blocking the use of RU-486 in the United States.

Sample Responses ───

Passage 1

CONCLUSION: *College students would do better in school if they would get more sleep.*

REASONS: 1. *Honors students claim that they sleep a lot.*

2. *The counseling center at our school says that students who stay out late at night are often the same students required to leave school because of poor grades.*

Before we all start insisting on more sleep, we should pause to take another look at the information provided to lead to this conclusion. What are the counterarguments, for example? Is it possible that staying up late frequently to do your work especially well might lead to better grades? And, just how much more sleep do honors students get? Would they do even better in school if they slept a little less?

Further, just what do we know about how the honors students were surveyed? Nothing at all! Finally, does the counseling center have any persuasive evidence that those who stay out late indeed are the same group of students who have the lowest grades?

These are just a few of the questions we would want to ask before we relied on the information in this passage.

Passage 2

CONCLUSION: *The warnings of health experts about high cholesterol and saturated fats have been effective.*

REASONS: 1. *Survey data reveals 35 percent less whole milk consumed, 34 percent less red meat, and 28 percent fewer eggs from 1977 to 1985.*

2. *Skim milk and whole grain consumption has risen during the same period.*

Before you accept the author's conclusion of dramatically improved health for the surveyed women, you should ask questions about what the study did not reveal. For instance, has the decrease in red meat consumption caused deficiencies of iron or other minerals in these women? Are these women selecting low-fat, protein-rich alternatives to compensate for the decrease in high-protein red meat?

Furthermore, fat from other sources should be considered. Whole grain bread is not a wise dietary choice when slathered with butter. Fried fish or chicken is not a healthful alternative to a lean, broiled steak. Decreased fat or cholesterol consumption in a few areas is not a fail-safe indication of improved health. High fat consumption in other areas and possible nutrient deficiencies are important considerations when assessing dramatic health improvements.

Passage 3

CONCLUSION: *The United States needs to pursue the possible use of RU-486, the French abortion drug.*

REASONS: 1. *A study in Scotland shows it is safe and causes fewer side effects than other available drugs.*

2. *The drug can save women from undergoing abortions and from confronting radical protesters.*

First, we should note that this reasoning advocates pursuing a new technology—a morning-after pill—and cites only its advantages. The writer omits possible disadvantages. We need to consider both advantages and disadvantages. What serious side effects might come from frequent, *long-term use* of the drug? What positive and negative effects might such a drug have on how men and women relate to each other sexually? Might people become less reflective about their sexual behavior? Would its availability make it easier for men to exploit women? Could its presence lead to less emphasis on "safe sex" and thus cause more AIDS cases? The advantages of the drug may well outweigh the disadvantages, but we need to be aware of both in judging the merits of the conclusion.

Furthermore, much relevant information is missing about the research. How were these women selected? Are they typical in terms of physical health? How many side effects are indicated by the phrase "fewer side effects"? How *severe* are the side effects? What do other research studies of this drug show? Getting answers to a number of questions would help us decide whether we want to fight efforts to block RU-486.

Passage 4 (Self-Examination)

The good news about the Year of the Woman was that rhetoric paid off. Fifty-four women now get to sit in the big rooms of the Capitol and ask the National Institute of Health, among other agencies, good questions. Also, women constituted a record 20.2 percent of all state legislators in 1993, much better than the 1992 high of 18.4 percent. Also, in terms of safety, women told researchers that the highly publicized trial of Mike Tyson resulted in their being somewhat or much more likely to report rape. And, on the health front, the good news is that research on women's health issues has improved dramatically in recent years, largely at the urging of female members of Congress and advocacy groups. In fact, in 1992, two bills— one that set quality assurance standards for mammography and another that established a program to prevent infertility in women with sexually transmitted diseases—were passed. Lastly, women fared well professionally; women between the ages of 24 and 35 earned 80 cents for every dollar earned by men in the same age category, meaning the wage gap narrowed. Indeed, 1992 was a good year for women.

13

What Reasonable Conclusions Are Possible?

By this stage you should be better equipped to pan for intellectual gold—to distinguish stronger reasons from weaker ones. In descriptive arguments, strong reasons will be persuasive evidence such as findings of a careful research study, a relevant analogy, an appeal to a reliable authority, or compelling examples. For prescriptive arguments, the strong reasons will be principles or descriptive statements you identify as best supported and most relevant.

Consider the following argument:

> It is time to end the divorce revolution we have been experiencing over the past 30 years. It has created economic insecurity for many mothers and caused untold numbers of fathers to walk away from financial responsibility for their children. In addition, countless children are experiencing the negative impacts of divorce. Thus, repealing no-fault divorce laws in cases involving children makes a lot of sense. By making divorces more difficult to obtain, more parents will stay together and work out their difficulties, reducing the divorce rate.

Should you urge your local congressman to support the repeal of no-fault divorce laws? Suppose that you checked the author's reasons and found them believable. Are there other conclusions that might be equally consistent with these reasons as the author's conclusion? The chapter summary will suggest several alternative conclusions that are possible.

Very rarely will you have a situation in which only one conclusion can be reasonably inferred. Consequently, you must make sure that the conclusion you eventually adopt is the most reasonable and the most consistent with your value preferences. The recognition that the reasons could provide support for conclusions different from yours should heighten your interest in any further tests or studies that would help identify the best conclusion.

☞ *Critical Question: **What reasonable conclusions are possible?***

Caution: Resist the temptation to see this critical thinking skill as just another name for the search for rival causes. The two skills are distinct. Their similarity is that both revolve around alternatives. Both remind us of the complexity of human problems. But the similarities end there. Rival causes are just what the name suggests, different stimuli for events, feelings, or behavior. We search for them only when an argument is causal in form. On the other hand, this chapter focuses on a more general potential problem when we reason. The reasons will probably be consistent with more than one conclusion. Whoever is making the argument will probably not acknowledge that the reasons may also support alternative conclusions. You, as a critical thinker, have to accept that responsibility.

Assumptions and Multiple Conclusions

Neither evidence attempting to support a factual claim nor a group of strong reasons supporting a prescriptive conclusion can be interpreted in only one way. Reasons do not generally speak for themselves in an obvious way. As we have seen many times, conclusions are reached only after someone makes certain interpretations or assumptions concerning the meaning of the reasons.

If you make a different assumption concerning the meaning of the reasons, you will reach different conclusions. Because we all possess different levels of perceptual precision, frames of reference, and prior knowledge, we repeatedly disagree about which conclusions are preferable. We form different conclusions from reasons because our diverse backgrounds and goals cause us to be attracted to different assumptions when we decide to link reasons to conclusions.

Sometimes a writer or speaker will mention alternative conclusions that can be reached on the basis of the reasons he has presented. However, *you* will often have to generate possible alternatives. To perform this creative task, try to imagine what different assumptions might enable someone to jump from the reasons you have identified to another conclusion. Remember, *many* possible conclusions can be made on the basis of most sets of reasons. The next two sections help you recognize the multiplicity of possible conclusions.

Dichotomous Thinking: Impediment to Considering Multiple Conclusions

Very few important questions can be answered with a simple "yes" or an absolute "no." When people think in black or white, yes or no, right or wrong, or correct or incorrect terms, they engage in *dichotomous thinking*. This type of thinking consists of assuming there are only two possible answers to a question that has multiple potential answers.

We encountered dichotomous thinking earlier when we discussed the either–or fallacy. This fallacy, and dichotomous thinking in general, damages reasoning by overly restricting our vision. We think we are finished after considering two optional decisions, thereby overlooking many options and the positive consequences that could have resulted from choosing one of them.

Dichotomous thinkers often are rigid and intolerant because they fail to understand the importance of context for a particular answer. To see this point more clearly, imagine this situation:

> Your roommate asks you to help plan her ethics paper. The paper is to address the questions: Should a person tell the truth? In her mind, the paper requires her to defend a "yes" or "no" position.
>
> You have learned that dichotomous thinking can be avoided by qualifying conclusions, by putting them into context. This qualification process requires you to ask about any conclusion:
>
> 1. *When* is it accurate?
> 2. *Where* is it accurate?
> 3. *Why* or for what purpose is it accurate?
>
> You then begin to apply this process to the paper assignment.
>
> Would you be surprised by your roommate's growing frustration as you explained that at certain specified times, in certain situations, to maximize particular values or objectives one should tell the truth? She's looking for "yes" or "no"; you provided a complicated "it depends on. . . ."

Rigid, dichotomous thinking limits the range of your decisions and opinions. Even worse, it overly simplifies complex situations. As a consequence, dichotomous thinkers are high-risk candidates for confusion.

The next section illustrates the restrictive effects of dichotomous thinking.

Two Sides or Many?

Before we look at several arguments in which multiple conclusions are possible, let's make sure you appreciate the large number of conclusions that are possible with respect to most important controversies. Here are three contemporary questions.

1. Do IQ tests measure intelligence?
2. Is the president's tax proposal desirable?
3. Should judges be elected or appointed?

At first glance, these questions and many like them seem to call for yes or no answers. However, a qualified yes or no is often the best answer. The advantage of *maybe* as an answer is that it forces you to admit that you do not yet know enough to make a definite answer. But at the same time you are avoiding a definite answer, you have formed a tentative decision or opinion that calls for commitment and eventual action. Once you recognize that you can never be certain how to answer a complex question, you can better accept the necessity of making decisions even when you know you are missing critical information or understanding. It's wise to seek additional information that would improve the support for your opinions, but at some point you must stop searching and make a decisions, even when the most forceful answer you are willing to defend is a "yes, but . . ."

Glance back at three questions that preceded the last paragraph. Ask yourself what conclusions would be possible in response to each question. Naturally, a simple yes or a no answer would be two possible conclusions. Are there others? Yes, there are many! Let's look at just a few of the possible answers to the first of these questions.

Do IQ tests measure intelligence?

1. Yes, to the extent that intelligence means sequential reasoning.
2. Yes, when they are given to children of the same sociocultural background.
3. Yes, if they are used for only elementary children.
4. Yes, when the IQ scores are highly correlated with measures of motivation.
5. Yes, but only in terms of the type of intelligence that is useful in schools.
6. No, if you define intelligence as that factor which leads to later success in one's chosen field.
7. No, if they failed to include data gathered orally.

Notice that in each case we added a condition that is necessary before their conclusion can be justified. In the absence of any data or definitions, any of these seven conclusions could be most reasonable. These seven are just a few of the conclusions possible for the first question. Thus, there may be many possible answers to a question, not just two.

Just for practice, try to suggest five possible conclusions for the third question: Should judges be elected or appointed?

Perhaps this conclusion occurred to you: *Elected, if it can be demonstrated that most of those who would vote understand the tasks of a judge well enough to make a choice consistent with efficient justice.* Or, maybe you thought of this one: *Appointed, in those states where the voter turnout in state legislative races has averaged less than 50 percent in the last ten years.* But probably neither of these appears on your list. Why are we so sure? Because there are an enormous number of possible conclusions for this question. It should be an unlikely coincidence if you had chosen either of these two from the huge list of possible conclusions. This greater number of answers is what we want you to grasp. Knowledge of the possibility of multiple conclusions will prevent you from leaping to one prematurely.

Searching for Multiple Conclusions

This section contains two arguments that point out multiple conclusions that could be created from the reasons in each argument. The intention is to give you some models to use when you search for conclusions. In each case, we will give you the structure of the argument before we suggest alternative conclusions. One clue to help you in your search is the following: Study the reasons without looking at the conclusion, and try to identify as many conclusions as possible that would follow from the reasons. You can always use the when, where, and why questions to help generate alternative conclusions.

> CONCLUSION: *There should be no law restricting access to alcohol.*
>
> REASONS: *1. Any young person who wants alcohol badly enough can get it, regardless of his or her age.*
>
>   *2. Many countries permit even little children to have a glass of wine with their meals, and these countries have not been negatively affected.*

Let's start by accepting these reasons as sensible to us. What do we then make of them? We have one answer in the conclusion of the writer: abandon all legislative restrictions on access to alcohol.

But even when we accept these two reasons, we would not necessarily conclude the same thing. Other conclusions make at least as much sense on the basis of this support. For example, it would follow that we should restrict access to alcohol, except in the young person's own home where the parents could guide consumption habits.

Or, alternatively, these reasons might suggest that we need much stricter alcohol statutes to prevent what is claimed in the first reason. Then, out of respect for the second reason, we would add to these new strict statutes a provision excluding wine consumption in the home. Not only are these two alternative conclusions logically supported by the reasons, they lead to conclusions that are quite different from the original conclusion.

CONCLUSION: *Congress should not decriminalize marijuana.*

REASONS: 1. *A group of British scientists has shown that smoking marijuana may cause serious brain damage.*
2. *Marijuana smokers risk decreasing their fertility.*
3. *Marijuana smokers often become heroin users.*

What conclusions are possible? One would be to decriminalize marijuana in one locale and observe the impact before making a national rule. Alternatively, Congress could sponsor research designed to develop a substance that would produce effects similar to those produced by marijuana without the possible side effects. Another possibility, based on a strong devotion to the value of individual responsibility, would be to permit pot to be sold in stores along with other possibly hazardous materials, the assumption being that those who may misuse the drug have a right to do so. Observe that all three of these conclusions are possible even if we accept the truth of the three reasons. Thus, the same reasons frequently can be used to support several different conclusions.

Productivity of If-Clauses

If you went back over all the alternative conclusions discussed in this chapter, you would notice that each optional conclusion is possible because we are missing certain information, definitions, assumptions, or the frame of reference of the person analyzing the reasons. Consequently, we can create multiple conclusion by the judicious use of *if-clauses*. In an if-clause, we state a condition that we are assuming in order to enable us to reach a particular conclusion. Notice that the use of if-clauses permits us to arrive at a conclusion without pretending that we know more than we actually do about a particular controversy.

When you use if-clauses to precede conclusions, you are pointing out that your conclusion is based on particular claims or assumptions about which you are uncertain. To see what we mean, look at the following sample conditional statements that might precede conclusions.

1. If freedom of religion is meant when the writer speaks of the loss of our basic freedom, then. . . .
2. If the birthrate continues to rise over the next five years, then. . . .
3. If it can be proven that most of those using the insanity defense today are truly mentally ill, then. . . .

If-clauses present you with multiple conclusions that you may wish to assess before making up your mind about the controversy, and they also broaden the list of possible conclusions from which you can choose your opinion.

Alternative Solutions As Conclusions

We frequently encounter issues posed in the following form:

> Should we do X?
>
> Is X desirable?

Such questions naturally "pull" for dichotomous thinking. Often, however, posing questions in this manner hides a broader question, "What should we do about Y?" (usually some pressing problem). Rewording the question in this way leads us to generate multiple conclusions of a particular form: solutions to the problems raised by the reasons. Generating multiple solutions greatly increases the flexibility of our thinking.

Let's examine the following passage to illustrate the importance of generating multiple solutions as possible conclusions.

> Should we outlaw those nudist beaches on the edge of our community? We certainly should. Look at the traffic problems they are causing and the hundreds of cars that have been parking illegally since the beach opened.

Once we change this question to, "What should we do about the traffic and parking problems?" a number of possible solutions come to mind, which help us formulate our conclusion to the issue. For example, we might conclude: "No, we should not outlaw the nudist beaches; we should have police vigorously enforce the no-parking rules and have the park service restrict the number of people allowed on the beach."

When reasons in a prescriptive argument are statements of practical problems, look for different solutions to the problems as possible conclusions.

The Liberating Effect of Recognizing Alternative Conclusions

If logic, facts, or studies spoke for themselves, we would approach learning in a particular manner. Our task would be to unplug our ears or have someone else, a teacher perhaps, unplug them for us. As our hearing improved, we would acquire the beliefs that we should have. Specifically, we would have that single identifiable set of beliefs that logic and facts dictate.

While we have tremendous respect for logic and facts, we cannot exaggerate their worth as guides for conclusion formation. They take us so far; then we have to go the rest of the way toward belief, using the help that facts and logic have provided.

A first step in using that help is the search for possible multiple conclusions consistent with logic and the facts as we know them. This search liberates us in an important way. It frees us from the inflexible mode of learning sketched above. Once we recognize the variety of possible conclusions, each of us can experience the excitement of enhanced personal choice.

We want to warn you that the rewarding feeling that often comes with generating multiple conclusions may tempt you to treat them as equally credible and to believe your job is done after you've made your list. But remember that some conclusions can be better justified than others, and the most believable ones should be the ones that most affect your reaction to the author's reasoning. Thus, after you have applied your creative-thinking skills to make your list of multiple conclusions, you will then want to carefully consider the credibility of each.

Summary

Very rarely do reasons mean just one thing. After evaluating a set of reasons, you still must decide what conclusion is most consistent with the best reasons in the controversy. To avoid dichotomous thinking in your search for the strongest conclusion, provide alternative contexts for the conclusions through the use of when, where, and why questions.

Qualifications for conclusions will move you away from dichotomous thinking. If-clauses provide a technique for expressing these qualifications.

For instance, let's take another look at the argument for repealing no-fault divorce laws at the beginning of the chapter. What alternative conclusions might be consistent with the reasons given?

AUTHOR'S CONCLUSION: *No-fault divorce laws need to be repealed.*

ALTERNATIVE CONCLUSIONS: 1. *If freedom of choice is more important than financial security, then we should not repeal no-fault divorce laws.*

2. *If it can be shown that repealing no-fault laws creates additional family conflicts by pitting parents against each other and forcing children to choose sides, then a better solution to the author's concerns might be to work toward reducing such conflicts, perhaps by encouraging greater use of divorce mediation instead of litigation.*

3. *If it can be demonstrated that no-fault divorce laws are not a major cause of increased divorce rates, or a much less important cause than such factors as increases in dual-career marriages or changes in parental roles, then the no-fault laws should not be changed.*

Many more alternative conclusions are possible in light of the author's reasons. Considering them would improve the quality of our response.

Practice Exercises

☞   *Critical Question:* **What reasonable conclusions are possible?**

For each of the following arguments, identify three different conclusions that could be drawn from the reasons.

Passage 1

A recent survey found that more than half of the $50 billion spent annually on automobile repairs was wasted. The survey covered 62 garages in seven cities. The survey found that many unnecessary services were performed and that the work was often of poor quality. In addition, only half the garages visited were judged "fair" in terms of the prices they charged.

What can be done to reduce this waste? A few well-publicized prosecutions might do wonders. Those who take advantage of consumer ignorance are the worst variety of thief. Consumers should make a special effort to see that such garages go broke by not taking sick automobiles to these rip-off artists.

Passage 2

In recent presidential elections, many more married than unmarried people voted for Republican candidates. This marriage gap is much greater than the more heavily publicized gender gap that favors the Democrats. Among high school students who expected to marry, a recent study found that almost 70 percent planned to vote Republican as soon as they could legally vote. Because most people are married, Democratic presidential candidates will have an uphill battle in future presidential elections.

Passage 3

When people are required to live together, there are bound to be numerous problems. Students all over our campus are moving out of their dormitory rooms because they have been uncomfortable in their previous living arrangements. The solution to this problem is to prevent the problems before they begin.

If the Housing Office would make it a practice to send out personality surveys and interest inventories before students ever set foot on campus, they could pair roommates who have something in common. The Housing Office is letting us all down when it permits the discomfort associated with trying to live with an incompatible roommate.

Sample Responses

Passage 1

CONCLUSION: *Those responsible for automobile repair rip-offs should be prosecuted for fraud.*

REASONS: 1. *More than half the annual expenditure on automobile repairs is wasted.*
2. *Well-publicized prosecutions of the guilty repair shops will serve as a deterrent and inform consumers as to which garages to avoid.*

The author's inference is but one of several that are consistent with the reasons. These include the following:

If the repairs are faulty because of undertrained mechanics, a better solution to the problem would be the licensing of mechanics.

If we assume that mechanics are urged to check automobiles not just for current problems but for impending ones as well, it's possible that the survey data was focusing on a narrow definition of "waste." Perhaps one could thus infer that mechanics should generally be praised for their long-range care of our automobiles.

The automobile is such a complicated mechanism that it's unrealistic to expect repair records any better than those reported in the survey.

Passage 2

CONCLUSION: *Democratic presidential candidates will have an uphill battle in the future.*

REASONS: 1. *In recent elections, more married than unmarried people voted for Republicans.*
2. *High school students who expect to marry in the future plan to vote overwhelmingly for Republican candidates.*

For the purposes of this exercise, we will overlook the deficiencies in the reasons. Accepting the reasons, we could infer several conclusions:

When Republicans emphasize family issues, they are especially attractive to married voters.

If Democrats run candidates who rely on the same type of media advisors as those hired by recent Democratic presidential nominees, they will probably lose.

If prevailing cultural images of home and children remain popular, Democratic presidential candidates are in trouble.

Passage 3

CONCLUSION: *The Housing Office is failing in its responsibilities to the students.*

REASONS: 1. *Large numbers of roommates have problems.*
2. *Discomfort among roommates is preventable.*
3. *Matching students' interests would make them more comfortable.*

To work on this particular critical-thinking skill, we need to assume that the reasons are strong ones. If we accept these reasons as reliable, we could conclude several things. For example, the conclusion already provided makes sense. But so do others. For instance, if the Housing Office has as a major goal encouraging interaction among diverse students, one conclusion might be that they are doing their job effectively already. Another conclusion that would follow from the reasons is that the legally responsible Housing Office should petition the legislature to permit an exception to the current laws requiring it to match students according to the diversity guidelines handed down by the Attorney General's Office. Notice that both alternative conclusions put the Housing Office in quite a different light compared to the negative portrayal it received in the original conclusion.

Passage 4 (Self-Examination)

It is time to do something about the damage that Title IX is doing to our athletic programs. It gives the appearance of fairness, when what it really does is create a very unfair and absurd situation.

The problem with Title IX is that it only looks to see whether the gender ratio among athletes mirrors the gender ratio among students generally, regardless of interest. So, even if many more men than women are interested in sports, colleges must strive to keep the gender ratio of their varsity teams the same as the gender ratio of the student body.

Following Title IX guidelines thus leads to bizarre situations in universities. The number of men's teams are reduced even though there is much interest in the abandoned sports, while women's teams are added that have a difficult time finding enough athletes to be competitive. Nationwide, men's swimming and diving teams are disappearing, and other sports like baseball and tennis are facing a very uncertain future. And, all this is happening when surveys consistently show that the subset of students who have the interest and ability to play intercollegiate sports is approximately 60 percent male. In fact, it is not unusual for a school to have eight times as many men as women come out for intramural teams and enough interested men to fill several basketball rosters.

Title IX is not providing equal opportunity. Instead, it is encouraging college administrators to manipulate their athletic programs so that men and women appear to participate in equal numbers regardless of their interest and ability to participate.

14

Practice and Review

In this chapter, we put it all together for you. We will begin by again listing the critical questions. This checklist should serve as a handy guide for you until the questions become second nature. When you encounter articles, lectures, debates, textbooks, commercials, Internet messages, or any other materials relating to an issue that is important to you, you will find it useful to go through the checklist and check off each question as you ask it.

Next we apply the critical questions by critically evaluating one position on a contemporary controversy. The major purpose of this discussion is to provide an example of a coherent application of *all* the critical-thinking steps.

We suggest that you follow the discussion with several goals in mind. You can treat it as a check on your understanding of previous chapters. Would you have asked the same questions? Would you have formed similar answers? Do you feel better able to judge the worth of someone's reasoning?

Question Checklist for Critical Thinking

1. What are the issue and the conclusion?
2. What are the reasons?
3. What words or phrases are ambiguous?
4. What are the value conflicts and assumptions?
5. What are the descriptive assumptions?
6. Are there any fallacies in the reasoning?
7. How good is the evidence?
8. Are there rival causes?
9. Are the statistics deceptive?
10. What significant information is omitted?
11. What reasonable conclusions are possible?

Asking the Right Questions: A Comprehensive Example

We first present a passage that summarizes one position with respect to the desirability of using racial characteristics as a basis for admitting students to professional schools. This section is followed by a lengthy discussion based on all eleven critical-thinking questions.

(1) Most professional schools have many more applicants for admission that the schools can admit. (2) Since access to education that will result in graduates becoming doctors, dentists, or lawyers is so valuable an opportunity, this access should not be decided by reference to the racial characteristics of applicants. (3) Yet many nonwhites argue for admissions policies that reflect "affirmative action." (4) Affirmative action is a euphemism for making admissions decisions on the basis of race. (5) Those for whom racial equality has been requested are now trying to be more equal than white applicants to professional schools. (6) If admissions and hiring decisions are illegal when they exclude nonwhites from fair consideration, then they should be illegal when they favor these same nonwhites.

(7) Affirmative action admissions policies for professional schools are disruptive, unnecessary, and even dangerous. (8) If one desires racial harmony, as I do, then affirmative action policies that unfairly aid nonwhites will be disruptive of our hopes. (9) Whites who are denied access, as well as their sympathizers, will probably be quite negative in their future attitudes toward nonwhites. (10) Affirmative action reminds us of our race and the fact that other racial groups are advancing at our expense. (11) If the objective that affirmative action is attempting to achieve is more nonwhite doctors, lawyers, and dentists, then a more acceptable option would be the creation of more professional schools.

(12) Those who support admissions policies based on affirmative action should be very careful. (13) If the goal of these policies is to bring representation in professions up to a level consistent with the minority's representation in the general population, then shouldn't the same reasoning be applied to other occupations? (14) Because there are a disproportionate number of nonwhites on professional sports teams, wouldn't it be a natural extension of affirmative action admissions policies to require coaches to reserve a certain number of team positions for white players?

(15) Affirmative action admissions policies are highly discriminatory. (16) How do admissions committees decide which minorities to discriminate in favor of? (17) Surely, many other groups besides nonwhites are treated unfairly in our society. (18) In all seriousness, why shouldn't women and poor, fat, ugly, or dirty people be given preference for admissions, since no one can deny that they have been victims of prior discrimination? (19) In fairness, we should either grant special admission privileges to all past victims of injustice or we should continue the current admissions policies based on merit.

(20) Nonwhites who are not qualified simply should not be granted scarce training slots in professional schools. (21) The United States Post-Secondary Testing Center has conclusively demonstrated that the average nonwhite applicant is less

qualified than is his white counterpart. (22) Yet we all know that under the guise of affirmative action, this inequity is encouraged. (23) For instance, a recent survey of law schools estimated that 80 percent of black law students admitted in 1990 would not have been admitted in open competition with whites. (24) Twenty percent of white law students, but only 1 percent of black and 4 percent of Chicano applicants, have undergraduate averages above 3.25 and LSAT scores above 600. (25) Thus, we are undercutting the quality of our professions by admitting relatively unqualified applicants.

What follows should serve as a comprehensive model of critical thinking. It proceeds in a step-by-step sequence based on the eleven critical-thinking questions. Though it will not offer a final conclusion, it will provide a reasonable basis on which *you* can make a decision.

What Are the Issue and Conclusion?

The passage denies the desirability of affirmative action admissions policies in the professional schools that train the nation's doctors, lawyers, and dentists. It is clearly opposed to the creation and continuation of special admissions policies for minority applicants. This conclusion is a response to the issue, "Are affirmative action admissions policies for professional schools desirable?"

What Are the Reasons?

Let's paraphrase the reasons that lead to the conclusion that affirmative action admissions policies in professional schools are undesirable:

1. *If racial discrimination is illegal, discrimination against whites is also illegal (sentences 2–6).*
2. *By highlighting racial characteristics, affirmative action admissions policies create greater hostility between whites and nonwhites (sentences 7–10).*
3. *An alternative method for creating more nonwhite professionals is the sponsorship of more professional schools (sentence 11).*
4. *The absurdity of attempting to assure that the proportion of nonwhites in each occupation is equal to the proportion of nonwhites in the work force can be seen if one will admit that competence in particular occupations may not be distributed identically to the distribution of racial characteristics in the population (sentences 13–14).*
5. *Class and sex are as important as race in determining social inequity. Thus, a focus on race perpetuates inequity while pretending to limit it (sentences 15–19).*
6. *Nonwhites admitted to professional schools by affirmative action admissions policies are frequently relatively unqualified. Admitting unqualified applicants eventually reduces the quality of professional services (sentences 20–25).*

What Words or Phrases Are Ambiguous?

In the arguments against affirmative action admissions, we look first for possible ambiguity that might weaken the reasoning presented, keeping in mind that we should be focusing on the author's major reasons. An important ambiguity pervades the entire argument concerning the desirability of affirmative action admissions policies. What precisely are affirmative action admissions policies? Notice how one's reaction to their desirability would be affected by the choice of either of the following alternative definitions:

a. *Active efforts to seek talented minority students in high school and then provide them with special training so they can eventually meet existing professional school admissions standards.*
b. *Encouragement of a racial quota which the admissions office is pledged to meet. Failure to meet the quota must be explained fully to the public.*

The first definition would find many more supporters because these kinds of affirmative action policies are more consistent with the competitive and individualistic values that predominate in our culture. That definition requires all applicants to eventually meet the same standards prior to admission. Yet we cannot tell from the passage what the author means by "affirmative action policies."

What Are the Value Conflicts and Assumptions?

One value conflict that has a strong impact on this entire debate is that between (a) *equality of condition,* defined in this instance as minorities receiving a proportional number of admission slots in professional schools, and (b) *individualism.* Those who attack affirmative action admissions policies tend to prefer individualism to equality of condition. They assume that it's up to each individual to earn the right to a position in a professional school without any help from the government. This value assumption links the set of reasons to the conclusion. Equality of condition would result in the type of proportional representation condemned explicitly in the fourth reason. A preference for equality of condition over individualism might cause one to reject the author's conclusion while granting both the truth of each of the reasons and the absence of any errors in reasoning. In such an instance, a strong preference for equality of condition over individualism might lead to the conclusion that affirmative action admissions policies are needed.

Other value conflicts that affect the author's reasoning can be derived from a closer look at individual reasons. The second reason reflects a value preference for social harmony over racial equality. The claim that affirmative action admissions policies will cause hostility between blacks and whites is based on the fear that whatever social harmony now exists would be disrupted by immediate movement toward racial equality. The sixth reason is based on the value assumption that excellence is a more important value than equality of condition. The alleged negative effect of affirmative action admissions policies is that future professionals will be less competent. The author is apparently less concerned about assuring proportional representation of minorities among professionals than he is about the level of skill exhibited by graduates of professional schools.

What Are the Descriptive Assumptions?

One descriptive assumption made by the author involves the use of *applicant quality*. In sentences 20 through 25, it is alleged that nonwhites admitted under affirmative action guidelines are often relatively unqualified. Yet the evidence that is presented is all based on a particular definition of application quality—namely, school performance records and their correlates. A broader definition of applicant quality that incorporated such applicant characteristics as verbal communication skills, willingness to empathize, or breadth of appreciation for the impact of lifestyle of clients on their behavior, might result in a very different attitude toward the worth of affirmative action admissions policies.

At least two other assumptions play a key role in shaping the attack on these policies. For the first reason to be true, we must assume that the past history of the treatment of racial groups should not be a consideration in determining the fairness of hiring policies. The author fails to recognize that rewarding certain representatives of a racial group may be the most effective strategy for compensating those who have been prior victims of racial discrimination. The author fails to consider the historical context in which affirmative action is occurring; thus, he perceives hiring and admissions decisions based to any degree on racial considerations as universally repugnant.

The truth of the second reason depends on the assumption that white reaction to such admissions policies will be molded by the predictably negative attitude of rejected white applicants. This assumption is questionable, because the white-dominated legislative bodies which have enacted civil rights and equal opportunity statutes apparently have sensed a growing commitment on the part of white voters to affirmative action policies. The author asks us to believe that this support for affirmative action will wither as soon as rejected white applicants become visible. Perhaps he is right, but the assumption he makes is only hypothetical.

Are There Any Fallacies in the Reasoning?

The third reason offers a proposed alternative method for increasing the number of nonwhite professionals. The alternative is in some sense a diversion. Many of the arguments for affirmative action admissions policies are based on a concern for the *relative* number of nonwhite professionals, rather than the *absolute* number. Therefore, sentence 11 is not an argument against attempts to increase the *proportion* of nonwhite professionals.

Two more blatant reasoning errors are committed in sentences 19 and 22. Sentence 19 commits an either–or error. The author gives the reader only two choices—either all victims of past injustice should be aided by affirmative action or no victim should be aided. That false dilemma makes little sense. Many alternative actions are possible. Helping a few who have been mistreated would make a start toward a fairer society. The demonstration effect of such an expression might encourage further efforts to compensate for past injustices. Alternatively, there may be many effective ways to help certain groups that do not require affirmative action. Some victims of past injustice may need affirmative action and others may need a different social commitment. Sentence 19 does not permit that flexibility.

Sentences 22 attempts to persuade through the use of the phrase "we all know that." But the author does not tell us *why* we should agree with most people that the subsequent generalization is accurate.

How Good Is the Evidence?

The fourth reason has an evidential problem associated with it. It is not a convincing argument to claim that such proportions should not be imposed on the professions because they are ignored in other key occupations such as in sports. This reason employs a questionable analogy. In sports there are clear performance criteria. Coaches and general managers will want players on their teams who can run faster, score more often, or serve more effectively. If a particular racial group has these skills disproportionately, they will predominate in a particular sport. However, there are no similarly clear criteria for what makes a competent lawyer, doctor, or dentist. Thus, the argument in the fourth reason that a criterion that would be unfair in sports is equally unfair in determining who gets into professional school is not convincing.

In at least one more respect the analogy in the fourth reason is flawed. The skills required to become a successful law or medical student are required in our educational system. There is no similarly strong link between schools and the development of sports skills. It is probable that there has been significant historical discrimination against racial minorities in our educational system and no similar discrimination in the process whereby sports skills are developed. Therefore, there is a basis for providing affirmative action help to racial minorities when they seek admission to professional schools; no corresponding basis is available to support the use of affirmative action in athletics.

The evidence used for the sixth reason is also flawed. Sentences 23 and 24 refer to a survey of law schools from which the authors infer nonwhite candidates are less qualified than white applicants for admission. However, we are told very little about how the survey was conducted. How many schools were surveyed? How representative were the schools? How did they define *quality*? For example, it would be helpful to know whether the schools surveyed had identical definitions of applicant quality. If their definitions are divergent, the use of a common definition in a later study might lead to very different inferences.

Are There Rival Causes?

Sentences 8 through 10 attempt to attribute increasing racial hostility to affirmative action policies. These sentences do not present a very convincing causal explanation. No other rival causes for increasing racial hostility are even examined. Certainly, the causal claim does not reflect a controlled study determining the effects of these policies on the incidence and severity of racial hostility. Sentence 9 is especially weak because it overlooks the positive effect on whites' attitudes toward blacks when whites are successful black professionals at work.

Are the Statistics Deceptive?

Sentence 24 provides us with data that appear to indicate the relatively poor quality of nonwhite law students. A couple of possible problems in this data should prevent us from immediately inferring that the quality of law schools and the legal profession would be diminished by affirmative action policies. First, he is comparing very different groups. The grade-point averages and LSAT scores of white law *students* are compared to those of nonwhite *applicants* to law school. Surely, those admitted would have higher average scores than would the total set of applicants. The author apparently set up the comparison of scores so that it would be most supportive of his conclusion. Finally, the study cited may mean nothing more than that nonwhite applicants are less capable *students* than are white applicants. It does not necessarily follow that affirmative action admissions would result in less capable *lawyers*.

What Significant Information Is Omitted?

One highly significant piece of information that would be useful to know in evaluating the last reason is the extent to which school performance predicts success as a professional. In the medical field, postoperative juries can assess the need for and quality of surgery. However, in most professional areas the definition of competence is vague. Consequently, in the absence of any consistent data relating professional competence to school performance, the common measures of applicant quality (on which so much of the argument against affirmative action admissions policies is based) are suspect. If someone could demonstrate a strong relationship between school and work performance by professionals, the last argument would be more potent.

What Reasonable Conclusions Are Possible?

Let's first list the reasons that we were least able to criticize. Next we will iden-tify alternative conclusions consistent with these reasons.

1. *If racial discrimination is illegal, discrimination against whites is also illegal.*
2. *Class and sex are as important as race in determining social inequity. Thus, a focus on race perpetuates inequity while pretending to limit it.*

Remember that we are looking for conclusions other than the one pro-vided by the author that are reasonable inferences on the basis of the reasons we could find in the passage.

One alternative conclusion is actually hinted at in the passage—work to make discrimination against blacks and whites illegal. Until the legality of such policies is determined definitively, there will continue to be widely divergent admissions policies by professional schools. An equally reasonable conclusion that could be inferred from the two reasons is that affirmative action admis-sions policies based on sex and class should be encouraged. Notice that this inference is quite different from the one reached by those who suggested the arguments, but it is just as consistent with their reasons.

Our critical discussion responds to only *some* of the facets of the controversy over affirmative action admissions policies. You may want to focus on other parts of the argument. Ultimately, *you* must decide which of the inferences to sup-port. Critical thinking can take you only so far. The final step is yours. You can feel relatively confident after following our question checklist that you have asked the right questions about the arguments and that you are better pre-pared to form a reasoned opinion of your own.

Index